BAAL SHEM TOV

RABBI YISRAEL BEN ELIEZER

VOLUME I

FAITH

LOVE

JOY

MYSTICAL STORIES OF THE
LEGENDARY KABBALAH MASTER

Compiled and Freely Adapted
by **Tzvi Meir Cohn**

BST Publishing
Cleveland, Ohio

Second Printing 2010

Collection, adaptation, introductory material by Tzvi Meir Cohn
Copyright© 2006 by Tzvi Meir Cohn
Cover Design by Aitan Levy
Cover Art by Shoshannah Brombacher
Printed in the United States of America

For information regarding permission to reprint material from this book, please mail your request to BST Publishing, Permissions Department at the address listed below or e-mail your request to info@bstpublishing.com

Attention religious organizations, spiritual conferences: Take 40% off and use our books as fundraisers, premiums or gifts. Please contact the Publisher:
BST Publishing
(216)752-0955
info@bstpublishing.com

ISBN: 978-0-9792865-1-3

Library of Congress Control Number: 2009936017
Library of Congress subject heading:
1. Hasidim — Legends. 2. Baal Shem Tov, ca. 1700-1760 — Legends.
3. Hasidism. 4. Mysticism Judaism. 5. Title.

BST Publishing
P.O.Box 221108
Cleveland, OH 44122
Tel: (216) 752-0955
info@bstpublishing.com
www.bstpublishing.com

Dedicated to the millions of Chassidim and their Rebbes, who for nearly three centuries, have cherished and passed these holy stories down to us.

יברכך יי וישמרך

יאר יי פניו אליך ויחנך

ישא יי פניו אליך וישם לך שלום

"May the L•rd bless you and guard you. May the L•rd make His countenance shine upon you and be gracious to you. May the L•rd turn His countenance towards you and grant you peace."

הרב אברהם אזדאבא

מרא דאתרא וחבר הבד״ץ דק״ק קראון הייטס

Rabbi Avrohom Osdoba

602 Montgomery Street

Brooklyn, NY 11225

(718) 771-8737

In 1977, I met Tzvi Meir HaKohen and he became my student for the next 2 years. Recently, I learned that he has been inspired to spread the teachings and stories of the Baal Shem Tov, the founder of the Chassidic Movement. For the last 250 years, Baal Shem Tov stories have fostered a heartfelt belief in G•d and added to the richness of Chassidic life. It is a well known tradition among Chassidim that telling Baal Shem Tov stories brings blessings of health, children and livelihood. I was very pleased to receive the manuscript of Tzvi Meir's collection of Baal Shem Tov stories, which were validated for origin and content by Rabbi Sholom Ber Chaikin. Some think that perhaps not all of the stories about the Baal Shem Tov are authentic and that the superhuman powers ascribed to him are unattainable. In response, there is a Chassidic saying that the stories could have been true and certainly the Baal Shem Tov did possess the powers as described. The goal of this book is to awaken the Jewish community to the beauty of a life imbued with Torah and Mitzvos which is the essence of the Baal Shem Tov's mission.

Wishing you success in your mission.

Sincerely,

Rabbi A. Osdoba

CONTENTS

INTRODUCTION

The most famous master of *Kabbalah*[1] and Jewish mysticism is Rabbi Yisrael ben Eliezer. Rabbi Yisrael lived from 1698 to 1760, and is known as the *Baal Shem Tov.*[2]

More stories are told about the Baal Shem Tov than about any other person in Jewish history. These stories have been passed down, primarily through an oral tradition, for over 250 years. More recently, books — and even more recently the internet — have been added as a means to continue the time-honored tradition of transmitting Baal Shem Tov stories from parent to child and from Chassid to Chassid.

The Baal Shem Tov stories are indeed glimpses of the life and culture of downtrodden, 18th century, Eastern European Jewry. However, to see the stories as *only that* is to miss their central role. In Chassidic life, Baal Shem Tov stories have formed the foundation of one of the most fundamental and important of Chassidic spiritual practices: telling stories about the Tzaddikim — the Jewish saints, as it were; literally, the "righteous ones" — the

---

[1] Jewish Mystical Tradition.
[2] Master of the Good Name.

great Spiritual Masters. These Tzaddikim led and guided the various Chassidic dynasties through the dark Exile of European Jewry, from the time of the Baal Shem Tov.

All Chassidim, irrespective of their particular allegiance — whether to Chabad, Bretslov, Belz, Satmar, Gerrer, Vishnitz, to name a few — share one common belief: that the basic facts of the Baal Shem Tov stories are just that — *facts*. There is an old Chassidic saying: "If you believe all of the Baal Shem Tov stories, you're a fool; if you don't believe any of them, you are a bigger fool."

Today, the stories and teachings of the Baal Shem Tov are as relevant as they were in the past. They inspire and guide us. They nudge us towards intensifying our service to G•d. They teach us through example how to live our lives with a joyful attitude. They enable us to experience the flow of love that emanates from G•d.

The Baal Shem Tov's contemporary importance is clear from a letter he wrote to his brother-in-law, a great Torah scholar, Rabbi Avraham Gershon of Kitov, who had immigrated to the Holy Land. In fact, the letter was never delivered, and remained with members of the Baal Shem Tov's immediate circle, until its publication some 30 years later. The authenticity of the letter is not questioned, and it appeared in a book entitled *BEN PORAS YOSEF*, which was written by Rabbi Yaakov Yosef HaKohen of Polonoye, one of the Baal Shem Tov's most devoted followers.

In this letter (called *The Epistle*),[3] the Baal Shem Tov describes an *Aliyat HaNeshama*.[4] The Epistle attests to two principal aspects of the Baal Shem Tov's legacy:

1) his unique path of Divine Service is of Messianic import; and

2) his ongoing mission is to bring the mystical dimension of Jewish religious practice to the entire Jewish people.

In the letter, the Baal Shem Tov writes:

"I entered the palace of the *Moshiach*,[5] where the Moshiach studies Torah with all the *Tannaim*[6] and the *Tzaddikim*,[7] and also with the *Seven Shepherds*)[8]. . . . I asked the Moshiach, "When are you coming, my Master?"

He answered me, "By this you shall know it: Once your teachings become publicly known and revealed throughout the world; and when your wellsprings have overflowed beyond what I have taught you and you have grasped so

---

[3] A freely adapted translation of the Koretz rendition appears in its entirety in the Appendix.

[4] Ascent of the Soul to the Upper Spiritual Worlds.

[5] Messiah.

[6] Jewish Sages of the Mishnah 10-220CE.

[7] Righteous people.

[8] Adam, Seth, Methuselah, Abraham, Jacob, Moses and King David.

that others too will be able to perform *Yichudim*[9] and Ascents of the Soul as you do. Then all the *kelipot*[10] will perish and it will be a time of favor and salvation."

To some extent, the *"wellsprings"*[11] of the Baal Shem Tov's teachings have been dispersed throughout the world by the Chassidic Rebbes who succeeded him. However, that the teachings of the Baal Shem Tov should be publicly known and revealed throughout the world and that the mystical dimension of Jewish religious practice should be brought to the entire Jewish people remain unfulfilled goals.

Although each of the stories in this collection has been printed in other collections of Chassidic stories, they were all originally oral tales. They have each been **freely adapted** and published in the service of the goal to hasten the coming of the Moshiach.

The stories presented in this collection include dialogue to give you a sense of how the stories actually sounded when they were being told. I used the Ashkenazi (Eastern European) pronunciation of the Hebrew rather than the Sephardic pronunciation used in Israel. The

---

[9] Kabbalistic meditation that unites one with the Holy One blessed be He.

[10] "Husk" in Kabbalistic thought, the aspect of evil or impurity that obscures the holy and good.

[11] Sources of continual supply or emanations of Torah.

reason is that the stories were originally told in *Yiddish*[12] with the Ashkenazi pronunciation of the Hebrew and I want you to get the flavor as well as the teaching(s) of the stories. For example, Shabbat is presented as Shabbos and Mitzvot is written as Mitzvos. I have also sprinkled in some Yiddish words or expressions to give you the feeling of hearing the stories from a Chassidic story teller.

Another bothersome question was which of my names I should use: Howard Martin Cohn (my English name); or Tzvi Meir HaCohane Cohn (my Hebrew name). I was born to a secular Jewish family and later in my life returned to the path of Torah and Mitzvos. When I was growing up, going to school and working, I was always called Howard. Later, when I became involved with Torah Judaism, my religious friends called me Tzvi Meir. The basis of the dilemma is that religious Jews might not be particularly inclined to buy a book of Baal Shem Tov stories compiled and freely adapted by some unknown writer with the name Howard Cohn. On the other hand, all other Jews, whether of the spiritual or secular persuasions, might not want to read a book written by some religious Jew whose name they often can not even pronounce. In the first edition I settled on Howard Cohn because the vast majority of Jewish people are in the second group of being more

---

[12] Jewish.

spiritually or secularly inclined and the main goal of the book is to publicize the stories and teachings of the Baal Shem Tov throughout the world. However in this, the second edition, I changed it to Tzvi Meir since I think it fits better with the nature of the series of books, this being Volume 1.

I would like to express my gratitude to many people who have made this book possible.

Rabbi Sholom Ber Chaikin for reading the manuscript of this book, checking for errors and catching various mistakes of fact and occasionally tone.

Aitan HaLevi Levy whose creativity, contributions and encouragement have been invaluable for bringing this book to publication.

Jill Brotman, my editor, for her important additions and comments.

Robert Burruss, my friend, for your insights and help.

My dearest wife Basha, for your constant support, assistance, encouragement and love.

My sons Daniel Menachem Mendel HaCohane and Avraham Schneur Zalman HaCohane for being wonderful children.

May G•d, blessed be He, shower blessings on all those who have helped in the preparation of this book.

Of course, none of this would be possible without Ha Kodosh Boruch Hu,[13] whom I thank "exceedingly with my mouth; amid the many I will praise Him."

---

[13] The Holy One, Blessed be He.

PREFACE

Baal Shem Tov literally means, "Master of the Good Name." How appropriate an appellation for Rabbi Yisrael Ben Eliezer, who was to become the founder of the Chassidic movement — the single most important religious movement in Jewish history! We know that he was born on the 18th of Elul in 1698, but little other verifiable biographical information has come down to us. Moreover, the Baal Shem Tov's life is so overlain with legend, it is difficult to determine what is true of the information we *do* have.

According to the stories, Rabbi Yisrael's parents were poor, righteous, and hospitable. When he was orphaned at a very young age, the Jewish community of Horodenka took him under its wing, fed and clothed him, and enrolled him in the local *cheder.*[1]

He is described as an unusually sensitive child, and quite early demonstrated a profound attachment to $G{\cdot}d$[2] and to nature. He often wandered in the forests and fields

---

[1] A Hebrew day school for young boys.
[2] It is a practice among observant Jews not to spell out the Name of the Almighty.

surrounding the village, and spent many hours there, alone, close to the natural world, talking to G•d.

At the age of twelve, he began working as the local cheder teacher's assistant. His job was to bring the students to and from school and to review their lessons with them. Later, he served as a *shamash,*[3] a *shochet,*[4] and worked as a laborer.

Unbeknownst to others, he was also devoted to Torah study and became extremely learned as a Talmid Chacham and Kabbalist.

The man who was to become the Baal Shem Tov so successfully concealed his spiritual and scholarly achievements that the great Talmudist, Rabbi Avraham Gershon of Kitov, vehemently opposed R. Yisrael's marriage to his sister, Chana. Rabbi Avraham Gershon viewed Rabbi Yisrael, who maintained a pretence of humble ignorance, as unworthy of the Kitover family name. They did, however, marry, and after they had wed, Rabbi Yisrael worked as a clay digger, a wagon driver, an inn keeper, and a healer.

In fact, the Baal Shem Tov (also know by the acronym the Besht) was part of a group of hidden holy men and mystics who worked among the "Jewish masses." Certain-

---

[3] A caretaker of the synagogue.
[4] A ritual slaughterer.

ly, in that place and time, the majority of Jews were ignorant of Torah. By moving among the common Jewish folk without revealing their status as learned men, these hidden "Saints" were able to relate easily to those they would later lead.

From his twenty-sixth to his thirty-sixth birthday, the Baal Shem Tov studied the deepest secrets of the Torah with Achiyah the Shilonite (from Shilo). Achiyah HaShiloni is described as a Heavenly teacher — one who was a Bibical Prophet and the teacher of both *Dovid HaMelech*[5] and *Eliyahu HaNavi.*[6]

During Rabbi Yisrael's years of travel as a hidden Saint, he had learned a great deal about folk remedies. Eventually, he combined his practical knowledge of herbs and healing with his mastery of Kabbalah, and his first public appearance was as a *Baal Shem* — the name given to a few, select, Jewish miracle rabbis that used mystical powers engendered by the Kabbalah, to heal the ill, ward off demons, and predict future events. The Baal Shem Tov was distinguished from the other Baal Shems because of his remarkable spiritual powers including the ability to see events from afar, predict the future, and look into someones previous incarnations to help those seeking relief from ailments of the body and soul.

---

[5] King David.
[6] Elijah the Prophet.

The Baal Shem Tov took to visiting the nearby towns and hamlets of Podolia, Volhynia, and Galicia, and began preaching the tenets of Chassidism. The most fundamental teaching of Chassidism, as taught by the Baal Shem Tov, is the omnipresence of G•d. The whole universe is a manifestation of the Divine. This manifestation is not an "Emanation" but a "Portion" of G•d; nothing is separate from G•d. Divine (G•d's) providence is a mantle over all. Therefore, everything in creation, including man, animals, plants and even inanimate objects are directly supervised by G•d.

It follows, then, that all things possess an inner spark of holiness — even something or someone we perceive as evil. Every person, no matter how far he or she has strayed from the ways of G•d, is capable of return; no sinner is damned. The Baal Shem Tov's teachings emphasized constant communion with G•d, and the enthusiasm and joy that are essential to an experiential relationship with Him. These ideas were not altogether new to Judaism, but the manner in which they were presented was little short of revolutionary. The Baal Shem Tov spoke directly to the masses of unlearned[7] Jews. Their task, he told them, was not to be something they were not — for example, learned Talmudists. Rather,

---

[7] Unschooled in Judaism.

their task was to infuse their daily lives with spiritual meaning.

The Baal Shem Tov taught that since G•d's providence extends to all of creation, everything is created and continues to exist because of His intention. As G•d is everywhere and in all things, all actions must be performed with an awareness of His presence, as well as with the love and joy that are integral to such awareness. One's goal in life should be to construct for the Holy One, Blessed be He, a habitation in this physical world. Through this, we will merit to bring the Moshiach, so that the world will be in accordance with G•d's plan.

The following was said by the Rebbe Maharash (fourth Rebbe of Chabad-Lubavitch 1832-1882): "The world makes three errors by thinking that telling stories of the Baal Shem Tov on *Motzoei Shabbos*[8] ensures one's livelihood. First of all, these stories are not to be limited to the Baal Shem Tov, but should include tales of all our Tzaddikim. Secondly, they should not be told only after Shabbos but at any time. And lastly, telling these stories not only ensures livelihood, but serves as a *Segulah*[9] to ensure we receive an abundance of blessings relating to our children, good health and success in our livelihood."

---

[8] After Shabbos ends.
[9] Spiritual Protection.

This teaching of the Rebbe Maharash is believed and acted on by all the various groups of Chassidim and is part of the reason I collected and freely adapted and published the stories in this book. By reading and telling these stories to others, you are promised by a long chain of Chassidic Rebbes that you will receive abundant blessings relating to your children, good health and success in your livelihood.

Please tell these stories to others and give this book to others in order to fullfill the requirement of the Moshiach for the Baal Shem Tov's teachings to become publicly known and revealed throughout the world, and his wellsprings (Torah from the source) dispersed throughout the world so that the Moshiach will quickly reveal himself.

SHALOM AND BLESSINGS

Faith Love Joy Faith Love Joy Faith Love Joy Faith Love Joy Faith Love Joy Faith Love Joy Faith Love Joy Faith Love Joy Faith Love Joy Faith Love Joy Faith Love Joy

G•d

Yisrael Ben Moreinu Rabbeinu HaRav Rav Eliezer KoesB
(presently in) Mezibush
Signature of the Baal Shem Tov

Chapter One

FAITH

The Baal Shem Tov taught that the power of faith is so great that even if a person believes in a physical impossibility, faith can accomplish miracles.

PERFECT FAITH

And then there was the time that Rabbi Dovid Leikes, one of the *Chevrayah Kadisha*,[1] was speaking with several followers of his son-in-law, Reb Mottel of Chernobyl (also known as the Chernobyler Rebbe).

Reb Dovid asked the followers of Reb Mottel, "Tell me. Do you have perfect faith in your *Rebbe*,[2] Reb Mottel?"

None of the men responded.

After a pause Reb Dovid persisted, "So nu?"

Finally, one of Reb Mottel's adherents came back with, "Who can say he has perfect faith?"

---

[1] The inner circle of the Baal Shem Tov's closest followers.

[2] Yiddish term for a Chassidic Master and leader of a Chassidic sect.

Reb Dovid nodded and continued. "My friends, let me tell you a story about faith. Once, several of us in the Chevrayah Kadisha spent a *Shabbos*[3] at an inn with the *Rebbe*.[4] As usual, *Seudah Shlishit*[5] went late into the night."

"The Baal Shem Tov told us of the mystical insights he had received while meditating, praying, and studying *Torah*[6] during that Shabbos. When he finished speaking, we *Benched*,[7] said *Maariv*[8] and then *Havdalah*."[9]

"Immediately afterwards," Reb Dovid continued, "we sat down together with the Baal Shem Tov for *Melava Malkah*."[10]

"After a few minutes, the Baal Shem Tov turned to me and said, 'Reb Dovid, reach into your pocket and take out a gulden, please, and buy us some mead (honey wine) from the inn keeper.'"

---

[3] Sabbath.

[4] Here, the Baal Shem Tov.

[5] The third meal, traditionally eaten on Shabbos before sunset.

[6] Twenty Four canonized scriptures of traditional Judaism. It consists of the Five Books of Moses, the Prophets, and the Writings. The Torah can also mean any spiritual text or idea that is connected to Torah Judaism.

[7] Grace after meals.

[8] The evening prayers.

[9] A ritual prayer recited at the close of Sabbath and other holy days that marks the separation between holy days and the ordinary days of the week.

[10] A meal eaten after the conclusion of the Sabbath that celebrates the return of the Shabbos Queen to heaven, where she dwells until the next Sabbath, when she returns once again.

"I was still wearing my Shabbos clothes and of course I never carry money on *Shabbos*.[11] Yet, without thought or hesitation, I reached into my pocket to take out the gulden, as my Rebbe had requested. And — the most amazing thing! I found a gulden in my pocket."

The disciples of Reb Mottel, after hearing this story, commented to Reb Dovid, "You know, that is really not that amazing. It's just another miracle story about the Baal Shem Tov."

"Yes. That is so," said Reb Dovid. "But the point of my telling you the story is not to show that the Baal Shem Tov does miracles. My point is that my faith in my Rebbe, the Baal Shem Tov, is so great that I didn't even think to question his request. I just reached into my pocket for the money. That it was there is secondary."

And so it was.

——————— • ———————

---

[11] It is a transgression of Shabbos to carry money on one's person.

Chapter Two

CHARITY

The Baal Shem Tov said, "G•d gave man the trait of being charitable to the destitute."

THE MEANING OF HOSPITALITY

Rabbi Eliezer and his wife, Rebbetzyn Sarah, outdid themselves in their observance of the *mitzvah*[1] of hospitality to guests. It was their custom to bring people to their home, especially those in need. They even employed local villagers to wait on the roads that passed by their little village of Okup, to invite travelers to their home.

On the *Festivals*[2] and every Shabbos, there were always many guests at their table. Rabbi Eliezer told stories of the Holy Jewish Masters, discussed the teachings found in the Holy Torah, and led the singing of the special songs for the day.

---

[1] Divine Commandment of the Torah.
[2] Rosh HaShanah, Yom Kippur, Succos, Pesach, etc.

The love and joy with which Rabbi Eliezer and Rebbet-zyn Sarah carried out the mitzvah of hospitality to guests did not go unnoticed in the Heavenly realms. It was decided by the Heavenly Court to answer Rabbi Eliezer's daily prayer. Every day he *davened*,[3] "Master of the Universe, please send someone to lead and inspire the *Congregation of Israel*."[4] In answer to Rabbi Eliezer's prayers, a very lofty Soul was selected to be sent into the world, to serve as a light and guide to the Jewish people. This holy Soul was to be raised by Rabbi Eliezer and his wife Rebbetzyn Sarah, who had no children, and were advanced in years.

However, the Angel known to all as the *Satan*,[5] stepped forward before the Heavenly Court and argued that while Rebbetzyn Sarah was certainly a Tzaddekes, Rabbi Eliezer was not worthy of fathering such a holy soul. He was still untested.

"After all," contended the Satan, "Rabbi Eliezer has not proven that he can withstand the most difficult test of all — loving a fellow Jew who scorns the path of his forefathers, that of the Holy Torah."

---

[3] Prayed.

[4] The Jewish communities in Eastern Europe were living in dangerous times and under difficult conditions.

[5] Angel that serves as the Adversary.

The Heavenly Court nodded in agreement. At that moment, *Eliyahu HaNavi*[6] came forward and said, "If Rabbi Eliezer must be tested, let me be the one to test him." The Heavenly Court agreed, and Eliyahu descended into this world.

The very next Shabbos afternoon, Rabbi Eliezer's guests were sitting at his dining room table enjoying a sumptuous Shabbos meal, when they heard a knock at the door. Rabbi Eliezer opened the door to a man in torn, dirty clothing.

The beggar carried a walking stick and a sack over his shoulder — a clear desecration of the Holy Shabbos, when carrying is not permitted. After muttering *"Guht Shabbos,"* the beggar barged in, dropped his sack and walking stick by the door, and sat down at the Shabbos table.

Rabbi Eliezer showed no sign of annoyance that this newest arrival appeared to be desecrating the Holy Shabbos. Instead, while Rebbetzyn Sarah prepared another place at the table, Rabbi Eliezer brought him wine for *Kiddush*[7] and two loaves of bread for *HaMotzi*.[8] The beggar mumbled unintelligible blessings over the wine and bread, and began to wolf down the food.

---

[6] Elijah the Prophet.
[7] The prayer said over wine to sanctify the Shabbos or Yom Tov.
[8] The blessing said over the bread.

Rabbi Eliezer's other guests were shocked and dismayed at the behavior of the new arrival. Carrying a walking stick and a sack is a clear desecration of the Shabbos. To eat and drink with barely a mumbled blessing — incorrect, at that — especially at the house of Rabbi Eliezer, was an outrage. They all watched Rabbi Eliezer to see how he would react. He showed no sign of displeasure, as he served his new guest.

That night, during the celebration of Melavah Malka, Rabbi Eliezer continued to personally serve the beggar, while telling stories of the Holy Rabbis.

The next morning, when the beggar was preparing to depart, Rabbi Eliezer gave him a donation and blessed him to have great success in all matters — family, health, and livelihood. As was his custom, Rabbi Eliezer escorted his guest to the door and accompanied him outside to the front of the house.

It was then that the beggar revealed himself. "I am Eliyahu HaNavi and I have been sent to test you. Because of your selfless love and your acceptance of others, you are worthy of having a son who will guide all of the Congregation of Israel and bring an infusion of G•dly light to the world!"

Within a year, the blessing was fulfilled, and a cherished son named Yisrael was born to Rabbi Eliezer and

Rebbetzyn Sarah. Later, Yisrael attained renown as the holy Baal Shem Tov. May his merits protect us!

And so it was.

————— • —————

Chapter Three

PRAYER

The Baal Shem Tov taught that cleaving to G•d is the master-key that opens all locks. Every Jew, including the most simple, possesses the ability to cleave to the words of Torah and prayer, thereby reaching the highest degrees of unity with G•d.

THE WAY YOU HAVE BEEN PRAYING IS JUST FINE

And then there was the time that a simple Jewish man, called Reb Yaakov, had a life-altering encounter with the Baal Shem Tov.

Reb Yaakov lived in a little village deep in the Carpathian Mountains. Although he was extremely poor and hardly a scholar, Yaakov had strong faith in G•d and was happy with his lot in life.

One morning, Yaakov was praying in the tiny synagogue of his village. The *Minyan*[1] had already finished their prayers and had left for work. On this day, Reb Yaakov felt a warm glow fill his heart, as he slowly and softly recited the prayers in the *Siddur.*[2]

Coincidently, just at that time, Rabbi Yisrael — the Holy Baal Shem Tov — happened to be walking in the countryside and passed the village. Being a mystic, the Baal Shem Tov saw a brilliant, G•dly light streaming out from the window of the tiny village synagogue.

"My L•rd, what is going on in there?" Rabbi Yisrael thought to himself.

He quickly walked over to the *Shule*[3] and looked in the window. There, he saw what appeared to be a simple Jewish man holding a Siddur and praying. The man, of course, was wearing his *Tallis*[4] and *Tefillin.*[5] Rabbi Yisrael went in, sat down, and immersed himself in the study of a Holy *Sefer,*[6] while he waited for the man to finish his prayers.

Hours passed. It was already early afternoon when Yaakov was finally done and removed his Tallis and Tefillin.

---

[1] The ten Jewish men needed for communal prayer.
[2] The sacred book of daily ritual Hebrew prayers.
[3] Synagogue.
[4] Prayer shawl.
[5] Ritual leather boxes containing verses of the Torah written on parchment, strapped to head and arm while praying.
[6] Sacred Hebrew book.

"*Shalom Aleichem,*[7] Aleichem Shalom," they greeted each other.

After speaking briefly, Rabbi Yisrael asked Yaakov, "Tell me Reb Yaakov, why were you praying so long?"

"Rabbi," he answered in a hushed tone. "I don't really know the meaning of the Hebrew words in the Siddur or even the right prayers to say. Usually I just start reading at the beginning of the Siddur and stop when the rest of the minyan finishes. But today, I felt particularly inspired so I didn't stop until I reached the end of the Siddur."

"Reb Yaakov, my friend," said Rabbi Yisrael. "Would you like me to teach you which prayers to say, and when to say them?"

"Oh Rabbi! I can't tell you how much that would mean to me. I've always wanted to know which is the right prayer to say. But I don't want to be a bother to you," replied the unassuming Yaakov.

"Oh Reb Yaakov, it wouldn't be a bother at all," responded the Baal Shem Tov. "In fact, I would be honored to teach you the prayers."

And so the two of them sat together for several hours, while the Baal Shem Tov taught Yaakov about the many prayers in the Siddur. They started with the morning

---

[7] Peace be to you.

blessings, the *Shachris*[8] prayers and the prayers said before and after eating. Then the Baal Shem Tov showed Yaakov the *Minchah*[9] and *Maariv*[10] prayers. They moved on to Shabbos and Yom Tov prayers. Rabbi Yisrael marked the separations between the prayers by placing small pieces of paper in the Siddur, with notes written on them to remind Yaakov about each of the prayers.

When he completed explaining the entire Siddur, the Baal Shem Tov bid farewell and left. He walked at his usual fast pace down the road leading away from the little village.

Yaakov was thrilled. He danced and danced around in circles while hugging his prayer book. Suddenly, he accidentally dropped the Siddur. The pieces of paper with the notes on them were scattered across the floor.

He stood, bewildered and dismayed. "What am I going to do?" he cried out. On one hand, he had always wanted to know the proper prayers and when to say them. On the other hand, he felt extremely embarrassed at the thought of asking Rabbi Yisrael to put the papers back in their proper places.

Finally, he decided. He gathered up the pieces of paper, and clutching his Siddur, started walking as fast as he could down the road after the Rabbi.

---

[8] Morning prayer service.
[9] Afternoon prayer service.
[10] Evening prayer service.

He could not see the Baal Shem Tov for quite some time. Then, Yaakov reached the top of a hill from which he could just barely make out the Rabbi, far off in the distance. "Whew!" he sighed in relief and started walking even faster. Just then, the Baal Shem Tov disappeared into a forest.

Yaakov followed him through the forest and suddenly found himself standing on a cliff, high above a wide, raging river. And there, by the side of the river stood the Baal Shem Tov. "Thank G•d," Yaakov thought, "I've got him now."

Just as Yaakov started walking down to the river, he saw the Baal Shem Tov remove his *gartle*.[11] Then, the Baal Shem Tov stretched it out, and walked upon it across the raging river. As soon as he reached the other side, he put his gartle back on, and continued walking away without even a backwards glance.

When Yaakov reached the edge of the river, he yelled out, "Rabbi! Rabbi!" But the roar of the river drowned out his voice. Without a second thought, Yaakov took off his gartle, stretched it out, and walked upon it across the river. As soon as he reached the other side, he started running as fast as he could after the Baal Shem Tov.

"Rabbi! Rabbi! Wait for me!" he yelled.

---

[11] A prayer belt worn by Chassidim.

The Baal Shem Tov turned around and was startled to see Yaakov. "Reb Yaakov, what are you doing here?"

Yaakov held out the Siddur and the pieces of paper. "Rabbi, I'm so sorry. I dropped the Siddur and all the pieces of paper fell out."

"But what are you doing *here*?" asked the Baal Shem Tov.

"Rabbi, I've come to ask you to please put the pieces of paper back into the prayer book."

"But Reb Yaakov, how did you get across the river?"

"Rabbi, I crossed on my gartle just as you did."

"You know," said the Baal Shem Tov, putting his arm around Reb Yaakov, "you don't need my papers. The way that you've been praying is just fine."

And so it was.

——— • ———

Chapter Four

HEALING

The Baal Shem Tov taught that it is necessary to travel to the Tzaddik, the great man of piety in one's generation. The Tzaddik will make his (the visitor's) prayer ascend to the heavenly realms (with his own) for the Holy One yearns for the prayers of Tzaddikim.

DISBELIEF

Shortly after her *Bat Mitzvah,*[1] the beloved daughter of a wealthy family suffered paralysis in her legs. Her parents took her to all the great physicians in Vienna, the city where the family resided. But none were able to determine the cause of the young woman's illness nor cure her.

The parents' hearts were broken. After lengthy discussions, the parents agreed that the father should travel with the daughter, and take her to every doctor — no

---

[1] Jewish girl reaches the age of maturity at 12 years old when she is responsible for her actions.

matter where he or she lived — until they found one that could heal her.

Over the next few months, they traveled by carriage from city to city, in search of a cure. During their journey, they stayed at inns along the way — typically run by Jewish innkeepers.

As it happened, each night the guests at these inns traded stories about their travels and even their personal lives. Naturally, the father of the paralyzed girl told about his search for someone to heal his beloved daughter. Many of the guests suggested that he take her to a holy Rabbi who lived in the holy community of Mezibush, deep in the Carpathian Mountains.

Of course, they were speaking of Rabbi Yisrael Ben Eliezer, also known as the Baal Shem Tov. The guests told the father that this Rabbi was a great mystic and Kabbalist. They said that the Baal Shem Tov had a reputation as a miracle worker, and that he could perform all kinds of wonders, including healing the sick, removing evil spirits, and traveling great distances in a short period of time.

Although the rich man lived according to Jewish law — as did most Jews at the time — he did not believe in miracles or miracle workers. He had been heard to say that miracle workers were charlatans who took advantage of the misery of their fellow Jews. Then, he would go on to describe how poor, needy Jews gave their last penny to these mountebanks, who imitated the prophets of old. And why did the poor Jews give these quacks their money? So that they would receive special blessings for healing, money, and children.

Weeks of travel and searching for a cure turned into months. Father and daughter journeyed with heavy hearts to the great European physicians — all to no avail. Finally, the father became so desperate that he decided to go to this Baal Shem Tov and ask for a blessing for his daughter.

They began the long journey to Mezibush. As they came closer to the region of Mezibush, Baal Shem Tov stories were invariably the main topic of conversation among guests at the inns where they stayed. With each story, the man's skepticism grew. By the time they reached the outskirts of Mezibush, he was really feeling like a fool. He decided that when he got there, he would just run in, ask the Baal Shem Tov for a blessing, and get right back on the road.

So the father drove directly to the synagogue of the Baal Shem Tov and stopped the carriage in the courtyard as planned. But when he opened the door and stepped inside, he found a long line of seekers waiting for the help and blessings of the Baal Shem Tov.

After standing in line for several hours, he realized that it would take many long hours before it was his turn. He thought of simply leaving, but they had traveled such a distance — and he didn't want to disappoint his daughter. Besides, where else could they go?

The petitioners waiting in line spoke quietly among themselves. Now and again, they spoke of the many miracles they themselves had known to have resulted from the blessings of the Baal Shem Tov.

The father struck up a conversation with the man standing next to him in line. The man explained what happens when one goes in to see the Rebbe. "Don't worry. I've done this before. Believe me, the Rebbe's blessings really work. Here," he said, "let me show you how to write a *kvittel*."[2]

The father wrote out a kvittel which read, "Dear Rabbi Yisrael ben Eliezer: Please give a blessing that my daughter Rachel bas Sarah be quickly cured. I also ask that she be blessed with a long, healthy, happy, prosperous life. Please bless her as well, to have a good husband, peace in the house and many happy, healthy children who follow the path of Torah."

After hours and hours of waiting, however, the father became increasingly irritated and upset. He found the

---

[2] A note in which the petitioner writes out his or her request.

stories of those who were waiting a bunch of distasteful nonsense.

Finally, it was his turn. He was escorted by the Rebbe's secretary into a room filled with holy books.

The Baal Shem Tov sat behind a desk looking intently into a Sefer.

At first, the man was startled by the holiness he felt in the room. But in a few moments he got used to it. Not knowing what else he should do, he said, "Rabbi, here is my kvittel."

The Baal Shem Tov looked up from the Sefer and directly into the eyes of the richly dressed man. After that, he turned his attention to the kvittel.

Then, in a somewhat sarcastic tone, the man said, "By the way, Rabbi, I am certain that this will be of help to you," and he placed a bag of gold coins on the corner of the desk.

The Baal Shem Tov looked up and said, "May your daughter, Rachel bas Sarah, with G•d's help, be completely healed. May she be blessed with a long, healthy, happy, and prosperous life. May she be blessed with a wonderful marriage and healthy, happy children that live according to the Torah."

Then, the Baal Shem Tov picked up the bag of gold coins and said, "To tell you the truth, I really don't have a need for this money." With that, he threw the cloth bag through the open window out onto the courtyard.

The father said, "Thank you Rabbi," and left the room thinking, "What a waste of time! And to throw money away, that's really disgusting!"

As he passed those still waiting in line, several inquired, "So? Nu? What happened? What was it like? What did the Rebbe say?" He just looked at them, without responding. "What a bunch of fools," he thought. Then he opened the door and rushed out into the courtyard to get back into his carriage and leave as quickly soon as possible.

Just as he stepped outside, however, he was startled to see his daughter jump down from the carriage, and run around the courtyard collecting the gold coins that had fallen from the bag of coins that the Baal Shem Tov had thrown through the window.

"Quick!" the rich man yelled to his daughter. "Get back into the carriage and let's be off! Why, he," pointing through the open window to the smiling Baal Shem Tov who was looking out at them, "will think that he is the one that healed you!"

And so it was.

———— • ————

Chapter Five

LOVE

The Baal Shem Tov loved all Jews, especially the simple Jewish masses, whose humble faith in G•d he often praised.

PERFECT TRUST

And then there was the time that the Baal Shem Tov showed his closest followers the holiness of simple, G•d-fearing Jews. The Baal Shem Tov was known to be particularly fond of simple, unlearned, G•d-fearing Jews. They, in turn, were his strongest supporters. Some of his closest disciples (who were typically great Torah scholars) could not understand their Rebbe's fondness for these unlearned people. They were often privately offended when the Baal Shem Tov sent them off to learn from such people about unquestioning trust in G•d and the love of one's fellow Jew.

The custom of the Baal Shem Tov was that the guests, who came to Mezibush for the Shabbos, joined him in

Shule at the Friday night *tish*,[1] and again the next day at
the Seudah Shlishit, which was eaten during the twilight
hours, late on Shabbos afternoon. By contrast, the large
midday Shabbos meal was set aside for the Chevrayah
Kadisha, the inner circle of the Baal Shem Tov's closest
disciples.

One Shabbos, a group of visitors, all simple Jews —
innkeepers, bakers, butchers, candlestick makers, wood-
cutters, water drawers, and the like — were at the synagogue. As was his custom, the Baal Shem Tov paid
special attention to these men and invited them to the
Friday night tish at his Shule. He shared with them the
Kiddush[2] wine with which he sanctified the Shabbos.
They ate from the two loaves of *challah*[3] over which he
had said the blessing of *HaMotzi,* made a few *L'Chaims*[4]
with the Rebbe and even had some herring.

The next day, the visitors ate the midday Shabbos
meal at their lodgings. They then returned to the Baal
Shem Tov's synagogue, where they poured out their
hearts beseeching and praising G•d, as they read from
the Book of *Tehillim.*[5]

---

[1] A communal dinner.
[2] The rite of sanctification of Shabbos or Festival.
[3] Braided bread for Shabbos and Festival.
[4] Drink.
[5] Psalms.

The Baal Shem Tov, as usual, ate the midday meal in a room above the Shule with his disciples. At the conclusion of their meal, he revealed secrets from the Torah that caused the disciples' hearts to fill with delight. The disciples thanked *Hashem*[6] for bringing them into the spiritual circle of the Baal Shem Tov.

But the feelings of a few disciples were clouded with resentment and jealousy. "Why does the Rebbe show favor to men who cannot understand his teachings?" they wondered.

The Baal Shem Tov sensed their thoughts. In a quiet voice, with eyes closed, he spoke. "Our Sages teach that in a place where a *Baal Teshuvah*[7] stands, the most righteous man, a Tzaddik, has no place. There are two paths in the service of the Creator: the first path is the righteous service of Tzaddikim; the second path is the contrite service of the Baal Teshuvah. The service of ordinary people belongs to the second path, for they are of lower spirit; they regret their imperfect past, and strive to improve their future conduct."

A quiet *niggun*[8] began around the Shabbos table, and those disciples who had doubts about the Rebbe's con-

---

[6] The Name — One of the ways Jews speak of G•d.

[7] One who repents and returns to belief in G•d and the observance of the Mitzvos (divine commandments).

[8] Melody without words.

duct realized that he sensed their thoughts. Soon the niggun faded away and the Baal Shem Tov opened his eyes. He looked deeply into the eyes of his disciples, one at a time. He told them each to rest their right hand on the shoulder of their neighbor, and to begin another niggun. After they had sung quietly for some time, he asked that they close their eyes. He then rested his right hand on the shoulder of the disciple who was seated at his right, and his left hand on the shoulder of the disciple seated at his left. The circle was closed.

From that moment, the disciples heard the sweetest of melodies, melodies that soared with the heartfelt requests of souls. *"Ribbono shel Olam* — Master of the World!" cried one voice, appealing to the Maker of the Universe in his own words, before davening to Him in the words of King David in the Psalms: "Examine me, Oh G•d, and test me; refine my heart!"

"Beloved Father!" another beseeched, and continued with the verse from Psalms: "Be gracious to me, Oh G•d, be gracious, for my soul trusts in You; and in the shadow of Your wings will I take refuge."

"Father!" came another cry. "Even the sparrow has found a nest for herself ..."

The holy brotherhood of learned disciples trembled as they heard these innocent prayers. They shed tears from their closed eyes, and envied the worship of these simple singers of Psalms.

The Baal Shem Tov lifted his hands from the shoulders of the disciples, and the music disappeared from their ears. He instructed them to open their eyes. Again they sang a niggun together.

(One of those present at that Shabbos table was Reb Dov Ber, later known as the Mezritcher Maggid. Years later, he recounted the incident to his own disciple, Shneur Zalman of Liadi, the Alter Rebbe, and told him that at that moment, he experienced a more intense love of the Creator than he had ever known before.)

When the singing had come to an end, the brotherhood remained silent. The Baal Shem Tov sat with his eyes closed in a trance of *dveikus*.[9] Then he looked at the men gathered around the table and spoke. "The music that you heard was the singing of verses of *Tehillim*[10] from the bottoms of the hearts of the simple people in the room below."

And so it was.

———— • ————

---

[9] Cleaving to G•d.
[10] Book of Psalms composed by King David.

Chapter Six

SHABBOS

The Baal Shem Tov taught it is a good practice for the physical man to rejoice on the Sabbath. Through this, the spiritual form can enjoy its attachment to G•d all the more.

SHABBOS JOY

The Baal Shem Tov called together his inner circle of disciples and announced, "Next Shabbos, I'm going to show you what Shabbos really is." The disciples were so excited they could barely wait for the next Shabbos to arrive.

Finally, the day came. They carefully prepared themselves by first immersing themselves in the *mikveh*,[1] then dressing in their special Shabbos clothes, and coming early to the Synagogue on Friday afternoon — long before the Shabbos evening prayers were to be recited. When

---

[1] Pool for ritual immersion.

Kabbalas Shabbos[2] started, they prayed next to the Baal Shem Tov, but didn't see anything out of the ordinary.

Just before the Shabbos evening prayers were to end, they noticed the Baal Shem Tov staring towards one side of the synagogue. When they looked in that direction, all they noticed was a poor, simple Jewish man praying intensely and with great joy. Still, it wasn't such an unusual sight at the Baal Shem Tov's synagogue to see someone praying like that. And other than the way he was praying, they didn't notice anything special about the man.

After the prayers, the Baal Shem Tov motioned for his close followers to join him in his study. They sat around a table next to the window. Because it was summer and the windows were open, they could see the man who had been praying with such fervor during the Shabbos evening prayers. They saw him enter his rundown house. They could even hear him greet his wife.

"Good Shabbos, my sweet wife," he said, joyously.

"And a restful and holy Shabbos to you, my dearest husband," responded his wife.

The Baal Shem Tov's followers could hear the husband singing *Shalom Aleichem*.[3] When he finished the song, he said to his wife, "Sweetheart, let us make Kiddush."

---

[2] Prayer for welcoming the Shabbos.

But the couple were so poor, they had no money for wine. So the wife placed two small rolls of bread on the Shabbos table and said, "My dear husband, we have no wine. Please make Kiddush over these two rolls."

"That is fine," he replied. "We'll make Kiddush over the bread. I'm sure the rolls will taste as delicious as the most special wine." They washed their hands with a blessing, said HaMotzi, and shared the two rolls of bread.

Then the wife spoke. "For the fish course, I've made something special." She got up and brought a platter of beans to the Shabbos table.

She placed a spoonful of beans on each of their plates and said, "May it be G•d's will that these beans have the taste of a wonderful fish delicacy."

As they ate the beans, their faces shone with delight.

The husband sang a few traditional Shabbos songs and then said, "Thank G•d we have everything we need to celebrate the holy Shabbos. Let's have the soup course, now."

They both took another spoonful of beans and smiled. "Umm, what a wonderful Shabbos soup," they remarked to each other.

---

[3] The ancient greeting sung to the two unseen angels who accompany a man home from the synagogue after Shabbos evening prayers.

Then they had a third spoonful of beans to take the place of the traditional meat dish and a fourth spoonful as a dessert.

"Come, my sweet wife, let us dance to celebrate the holy Shabbos." So they both got up and began to dance about their Shabbos table and laughed and laughed.

Each of the disciples standing with the Baal Shem Tov felt a warm glow rise within. The Baal Shem Tov whispered, "You are each experiencing Shabbos joy, similar to the joy this holy couple has been feeling. You should realize that it is not the simple food that they tasted, but the Shabbos itself."

And so it was.

———— • ————

Chapter Seven

BLESSINGS

The Baal Shem Tov helped to bring G•d's justice into the world.

THE WEDDING BLESSINGS

A Jewish innkeeper had hired a teenage boy and a teenage girl. The boy and the girl were both orphans. Over time, they developed special feelings for each other. The special feelings were apparent to everyone who saw them together. The innkeeper promised that he would help them to get married, after they had worked for him a few years longer.

One day, the boy saw the innkeeper's wife scream at the girl. When the innkeeper's wife struck the girl, the boy screamed at the woman, and even raised his hand to her. The innkeeper, hearing the screams, rushed to see what the commotion was about. As luck would have it, it was just at the moment that he arrived, that the servant boy raised his hand against the innkeeper's wife.

The innkeeper ran over and grabbed the boy's hand. Then he started screaming at both of the orphan servants. When the boy spoke up and tried to explain that the innkeeper's wife had hit the girl, the innkeeper grew even angrier. He told them to pack their bags and get out of his inn. As the young couple walked out into the bitterly cold Ukrainian winter, the innkeeper yelled, "And I never want to see your ugly faces again!"

The young couple used all of their savings to buy a rickety old sled and a tired old horse. They traveled from town to town, looking for a place to settle. But, no luck. After weeks of traveling in freezing temperatures across the Ukrainian countryside, they had no food and no money. They didn't know where to go.

The day came when they were so weak and tired, they gave up. The cold filled their famished bodies. They lay unconscious in the sled, which the starving horse continued to drag down the road.

Late in the afternoon, the horse stopped next to a small fire around which a group of the Baal Shem Tov's disciples sat.

Earlier that morning, the Baal Shem Tov had told Alexei, his wagon driver, to prepare the sled for a trip.

Then, he had invited a group of his closest followers to accompany him on his travels — to an undisclosed destination. The disciples loved to join their Rebbe on such mysterious and magical trips.

As was often the case, once the sled had left Mezibush, Alexei put down the reins. He took a few sips from a bottle of whiskey, snuggled up under a heavy blanket, and went to sleep for the duration of the trip. The horse and sled seemed to fly through the air and traveled a great distance in a short period of time.

On this trip, and in this fashion, the Baal Shem Tov and his disciples had traveled from early morning until afternoon. The disciples were desperately cold, and they had quietly discussed among themselves how much longer it would be before they reached an inn — where they could warm up, eat, and, hopefully, spend the night. All of a sudden, the Baal Shem Tov announced that they would stop and daven Mincha beside the road.

The disciples wanted to continue on to the nearest inn, but the Baal Shem Tov insisted that they stop right there. They were all so cold, they decided to build a fire to warm themselves.

The fire was already blazing when the disciples completed the afternoon prayers. Then, almost out of nowhere, they saw a small sled pulled by a haggard horse slowly approaching their fire. The sled was covered in a sheet of white frost.

When they looked closer, they saw a teenage boy and girl huddled together under a pile of blankets. Their eyes were open and they looked as though they were staring through the layer of frost that covered their faces.

The disciples rushed over, and pulled the young couple from the sled. They wrapped the blankets around them and placed them on the ground next to the fire, in hopes of being able to "thaw out" their already blue bodies. When they regained consciousness, the disciples helped them sip from cups of hot tea and brandy.

After recovering, the boy and girl told the Baal Shem Tov and his followers that their names were Shlomo and Rivka and that they worked for a Jewish innkeeper and had been planning to get married. Then they told of the events that had lead to their being nearly frozen in the sled.

When they had finished telling their story, the Baal Shem Tov said, "A young man and a young woman cannot travel together like this without being married. We are going to make a *chasana*."[1] Without further discussion, they all got back into their sleds and started traveling.

---

[1] A wedding.

Within a few hours, the two sleds had arrived at an inn. When the innkeeper heard the sounds of their arrival, he rushed out to greet the group of Chassidim. As he was instructing them regarding where they should put the sleds and bed down and feed the horses, he noticed Shlomo and Rivka.

"What are they doing here? They will not step foot in my inn!" he shouted.

The innkeeper's wife, hearing her husband's yelling, came outside and stood next to her husband. "Get away from here, you dirty little brats," she screamed. "Please," said the Baal Shem Tov, "We want to have a chasana at your inn."

"And who are the *chosson*[2] and the *kallah*,[3] may I ask?" queried the innkeeper.

"Why, this young couple," answered the Baal Shem Tov.

The innkeeper and his wife began to laugh uproariously. Then, the innkeeper suddenly became serious and said, "They will get married here — over my dead body."

The Baal Shem Tov took the innkeeper aside and spoke to him in a quiet voice. As the two men walked into

---

[2]Groom.
[3] Bride.

the inn, the disciples saw the Baal Shem Tov pour a pile
of gold coins on the table.

Immediately, the innkeeper called to his wife, and they
began planning a wedding party for the young couple. The
Baal Shem Tov reminded the innkeeper, "Don't forget. We
want the best wine from your wine cellar for the celebration."

The next afternoon, there was a gala wedding at the
inn. Word of the chasana passed through the nearby
town, and the townsfolk flocked to the celebration. The
Baal Shem Tov was the officiating Rabbi and his disciples
took care of the other details of the marriage ceremony.

After the couple had been married under the *Chupah*,[4]
the guests danced and ate and drank their fill. Then the
Baal Shem Tov, sitting at a table with his followers said,
"It is only right that the chosson and kallah receive gifts
to begin their life together." The guests cheered and
clapped their approval.

When they quieted down, the Baal Shem Tov continued, "And for my gift, I would like to give the chosson and
the kallah this beautiful inn."

After a momentary silence, the innkeeper and his wife
laughed so hard they could barely stand.

---

[4] Wedding canopy.

Then one of the followers, Reb Dov Ber (later known as the Mezritcher Maggid) chimed in, "And I would like to give them the flour mill down by the river."

"I will give the stables and horses by the inn," piped up Reb Ze'ev Kotses, another Chassid.

"And I will give the wine cellar in the inn," added another disciple.

Everyone at the wedding party turned to look at the innkeeper and his wife, and the Baal Shem Tov said, "And what about you innkeeper? What gift will you give to the newly married couple?"

"Oh, I will give them five rubles," said the innkeeper.

"Please," said the Baal Shem Tov. "That is not enough for a couple that has just had a big wedding at your inn."

"You are right," said the innkeeper. "I will give them the five thousand rubles of rent money that the Duke just collected from his land holdings."

The innkeeper's wife followed his words with, "And they can live in the old broken-down house at the end of town."

When the wedding guests murmured complaints about her stinginess, she said, "Okay, I will give the kallah the big diamond broach the Duke's wife always wears."

Then the wedding party benched and recited the *Sheva Brochos*[5] that are said after a wedding meal. The Baal Shem Tov quickly wrapped all the leftover food and drink into the table cloths that he had purchased from the innkeeper. The disciples put the leftovers into the little sled along with the newly-wedded choson and kallah.

The Baal Shem Tov and the disciples got into their sled. Just before they departed, the Baal Shem Tov said to the young couple, "I give you a blessing that all of the blessings we bestowed on you will be fulfilled, and that you live long, healthy, happy lives both physically and spiritually and that you have children that follow in the ways of our holy Torah."

The newlyweds, still wearing their wedding clothes, got into their sled and started off along the road. At first, they were elated with the turn of events. They had been thrown out of the inn and, then, they had married at the very same inn! They felt as though they had just awakened from a wonderful dream.

But after traveling a few hours, it dawned on them that they still had no place to go. And they still had no money. They felt worse, with the growing realization that they were in the same situation as before they had met Baal Shem Tov — except, of course, that now they were

---

5 Seven blessings traditionally said after a wedding meal.

married and had food in the sled. As the hours passed and the tired old horse pulled their sled along a frozen Ukrainian road, they became more and more despondent.

Suddenly, the couple noticed an odd shape in the snow, by the side of the road. It almost looked like a person! They got off the sled for a better look. "My G•d, it's a young nobleman," said Rivka. His skin was blue and icicles were forming on his beard. "Quick Shlomo," she instructed, "build a fire!"

Shlomo and Rivka covered the young nobleman with blankets and got a fire blazing. When he regained consciousness, they gave him a drink of whiskey and fed him from the leftover food of the wedding.

As he slowly came back to himself, the young nobleman related how he had had an accident, while hunting. He had fallen from his horse and his horse had run away.

Before he finished relating the story, the three of them heard the trumpeting of a hunting horn. Shortly thereafter, a servant of the young nobleman's father, the Duke, came riding up in search of the young man. As soon as he set eyes on him, the servant signaled for a carriage. The Duke's son got into the carriage, and they left without thanking or even acknowledging the newlyweds.

The Duke and the Duchess were hosting an extremely somber party to celebrate the collection of the Duke's rents. They and their entourage had returned from hunting that afternoon, only to learn that their son — their only child — was missing.

When the carriage carrying the young nobleman arrived at the castle, he was brought to his parents immediately. As he entered the party room, everyone cheered and breathed a sigh of relief. The boy was still in shock, and was taken to his room to recover. After some time, however, he came to himself and recalled how he had fallen from his horse and been saved by a young couple.

The young man ran down to his parents to inquire about the couple that had saved his life. Everyone had forgotten about them.

"Quick! Find the couple and bring them here," the Duke instructed his servants. The servants rushed off, and found the couple. (Their fire and food gone, Shlomo and Rivka had been sitting in their sled under blankets, once more unsure of their fate.) They were brought to the castle and given a heroes' welcome.

The Duke questioned the couple, and learned of their being thrown out of the inn (which coincidently belonged to the Duke), their meeting with a strange rabbi called the Baal Shem Tov, their wedding, and their finding the Duke and Duchess's son.

The Duke, the Duchess, their servants, and their guests were thrilled that the young man had been miraculously saved and had come to no harm. The music played and the liquor flowed, as they all crowded around the young couple, thanking them again and again.

Someone cried, "Let us help the newlyweds begin their life together with some gifts!" The Duke jumped up and said, "I am giving the newlyweds my inn, which is being run by that miserable innkeeper and his wife!"

When one of the royal party suggested that they be given the stables, the horses, and the wine cellar at the inn, the Duke responded, "Absolutely! all of that will be included."

Then another guest proposed, "What about the mill by the river?"

"Of course I agree. They are beautiful young people, and it is a wonderful idea," agreed the Duke.

"But won't they need cash?" offered the Duke's brother.

"Why, here is five thousand rubles — the rent I just collected from my tenants." And the Duke thrust a bag of gold coins into Shlomo's hand.

Then the Duchess removed her famous diamond broach and pinned it onto Rivka's wedding gown. She effused, "You are the most beautiful of all brides, and this is the least I can offer to thank you for giving me back my only son." Then she hugged Rivka and began to weep.

"But what about the innkeeper and his wife?" Rivka asked. "Where will they live?"

"Oh, we will give them the broken-down house at the end of the town," answered the Duke's wife.

And so it was.

———— • ————

Chapter Eight

REPENTANCE

The Baal Shem Tov taught that G•d allows each person the opportunity to atone for their errors.

TWO CANDLES ARE ENOUGH

And then there was the time that Yankel, a hard working wagon driver had the worst experience of his life. Yankel was a simple Jew. He could barely read the Hebrew prayer book — much less study the Holy Torah. Nevertheless, he tried his best to fulfill the mitzvahs. He often thought to himself that surely G•d would look kindly on his efforts.

One Friday afternoon, Yankel was returning in his wagon from a trip to take someone to the neighboring village. The road was muddy, and he made little progress. After a while, he started to worry that he might not make it home before the beginning of the holy Shabbos. He tried to encourage the horse to go faster. As it got later, he even took the whip to his horse! But then he thought, "What's the use? I'm just too far away."

He considered spending Shabbos in the forest, but quickly abandoned that idea. "It's too dangerous in the woods at night, what with the wild animals and the roaming bandits." So he continued on his way.

When he finally reached his small village, the streets were quiet. The women were getting ready for the Shabbos meal or putting children to bed. No doubt, the men had already gone to the synagogue for Friday night prayers.

Yankel quickly un-harnessed his horse from the wagon and put it in the small barn next to his home. As he walked towards the house, he looked in the window and saw that the Shabbos candles were already lit!

He opened the door. His anxious wife came running and threw her arms around him. "Yankel, I was so worried about you. Where have you been?"

With that, Yankel broke down. "I've committed a terrible sin. I've desecrated the holy Shabbos." He sobbed as he told her the whole story.

She tried to comfort him. "Yankel, a Jew should not be upset on Shabbos. You didn't intentionally break Shabbos: You had no choice. When Shabbos ends, you will talk with the Rabbi."

His wife's words made Yankel feel better, so he changed into his Shabbos clothes. He recited the evening prayers, made Kiddush over the wine, and sat down with his wife for the Shabbos dinner.

The next night, as soon as Shabbos had ended, Yankel hurried to see the Rabbi. He related his story in a sad and broken voice.

The Rabbi reassured him. "Yankel, don't despair. The Almighty is merciful. Next Friday, bring two candles to the synagogue in honor of Shabbos. G•d will surely forgive you."

On Friday, Yankel brought two large candles to the synagogue. He arrived early. The synagogue was empty except for Yechiel Michel of Zlotchov — a devoted follower of the Holy Baal Shem Tov. Yechiel watched as Yankel placed two large candles on the *chazzan's*[1] stand and lit them.

"Yankel, what are you doing?" he asked. Yankel told him the whole story of how he had transgressed the Shabbos and how the Rabbi had instructed him to bring the two candles.

Yechiel was outraged. "Two candles to atone for violating the holy Shabbos!" he screamed. "Are you crazy?"

---

[1] Prayer leader.

Yankel was crushed. To make matters worse, at that very moment, the door to the Shule opened, and the flames on Yankel's candles were blown out by a gust of wind. Yankel felt like a broken man. G•d had rejected his repentance!

So Yankel returned to the Rabbi and told him what had happened. The Rabbi suggested that he visit the Baal Shem Tov and ask his advice. Early the next day, on Sunday morning, Yankel left for Mezibush in his wagon with his old horse leading the way.

As soon as he arrived, he had *Yichidus*[2] with the Baal Shem Tov. Yankel's eyes filled with tears, as he told him the whole story.

The Baal Shem Tov responded in a warm, soft voice. "Reb Yankel, your Rabbi gave you an appropriate atonement. Next Friday, take two candles to the synagogue and light them. I assure you that the candles will burn brightly and that your repentance will be accepted by G•d."

Yankel was relieved and thanked the Baal Shem Tov.

"And could you kindly do me a favor?" asked the Baal Shem Tov. "When you return to your village, would you please give this letter to my Chassid, Yechiel Michel?" Of course, Yankel said that he would.

---

[2] Private audience with Rebbe.

When Yankel returned home, he delivered the Baal Shem Tov's letter to Yechiel Michel. Yechiel opened the envelope right away. Inside, he found an invitation from the Baal Shem Tov to spend the next Shabbos as his guest in Mezibush. Yechiel was thrilled.

The following Thursday morning, Yechiel harnessed his horse to his wagon and departed for Mezibush. Although the journey normally took only half a day, Yechiel took a wrong turn and found himself lost in a deep forest. As he searched for the right way, it began to snow. Soon, the snow was falling so thickly, he could barely see his horse, who trotted very slowly down the snowy, muddy road. Yechiel was forced to spend the night in the forest, huddled in his wagon.

Friday morning it was still snowing. Yechiel was cold and hungry, and he began to think that he would not reach Mezibush before the Shabbos. As the hours passed, he was beside himself with worry. "If I stay out here, I can easily freeze to death. And what about the wild animals and the robbers? But if I drive the wagon into Mezibush, I'll desecrate Shabbos."

About an hour before sundown and the beginning of Shabbos, it finally stopped snowing. Yechiel took the whip to his horse, so that he would move more quickly. Shortly thereafter, he could see Mezibush in the distance. And just seconds before the sun set, Yechiel pulled up in front of the inn where he was to stay.

Yechiel quickly changed into his Shabbos clothes and rushed to the Baal Shem Tov's synagogue. "But," he wondered, "how can I stand in the presence of the Rebbe, without having gone to the mikveh?" So Yechiel spent the entire Shabbos sitting in the corner at the back of the synagogue, very depressed. To make matters worse, the Baal Shem Tov never even glanced his way.

At the end of Shabbos, the Baal Shem Tov motioned to Yechiel and asked him to join him in his study. After the Baal Shem Tov had closed the door, he said, "It was decreed in Heaven that you should feel the pain and anguish that Yankel the wagon driver felt, when he couldn't get home in time for Shabbos. It was only through my intervention that you were saved from transgressing Shabbos. This is a very important lesson for you to learn. If someone truly regrets his transgression, then two candles are enough for a proper atonement."

And so it was.

———— • ————

Chapter Nine

MONEY

You open Your Hand and fulfill the will of every living being.[1]

FERVENT PRAYER

And then there was the time that the Baal Shem Tov and several of his closest followers had been traveling by horse and wagon for several days. After another long day of travel, they were all cold, tired and famished.

They came upon a secluded village, and much to their relief, the Baal Shem Tov announced that they would stop there for the night. He went on to say, "I think that we will receive a large amount of *tzedaka*[2] from one of the villagers."

The followers looked at each other and rolled their eyes in disbelief. None of them had ever heard of this out-of-the-way hamlet. Moreover, the houses in the village

---

[1] Psalm 145:16.
[2] Charity.

appeared so rundown, they were skeptical that any of the villagers would have any money to give them. Besides, they were far from Mezibush, and it seemed unlikely that the villagers would have heard of their wonderful Rebbe, the Baal Shem Tov.

The horse, also weary, slowly pulled the wagon into the village. On its own, it came to a stop in front of the dilapidated house of a poor Jewish family. With a sigh of relief, they all got down from the wagon and knocked on the door. The woman of the house gave them a warm welcome and asked them all to come in and sit down. When they entered, they looked around and saw that the interior of the two-room house was as shabby as the exterior. They all sat down around the one table in the middle of the room.

After a few minutes the Baal Shem Tov spoke. "Rebbetzyn, we cannot thank you enough for your hospitality. We have been traveling all day and are still cold and very hungry."

She felt sorry for them, so she heated water for tea and gave them the little bread that she had been saving to feed her children. This did not go unnoticed by the children, who were wearing rags. They stared at the group of strangers eating the meager dinner their mother had originally prepared for them.

The children began crying. "Mama we're hungry. Please give us some food to eat." The mother was heartsick, because after feeding the men, there was no food for her children. The Baal Shem Tov's followers were mortified by the scene unfolding before their eyes. How could they have taken food from children? They looked with questioning eyes to the Baal Shem Tov, but he seemed unmoved by the children's cries.

Just then, the man of the house, Reb Moshe, opened the door. Reb Moshe sold liquor, and had just returned from an unsuccessful business trip. He had tried to purchase a keg of whiskey on credit, but he had been turned down because he still owed money to the whiskey merchant from previous purchases.

Reb Moshe was shaken when he saw his children crying with hunger, his wife upset, and a group of strangers sitting around his table eating his family's last morsel of food.

Immediately, the Baal Shem Tov stood up and introduced himself and his students to Reb Moshe. At first, Moshe was flattered that the famous Baal Shem Tov had come to visit him, of all people. But then the Baal Shem Tov said, "My dear friend, we've come all this way to collect eighteen rubles from you. It is for a very good cause, and I'm sure you will be blessed for giving this tzedakah."

"Eighteen rubles!" gasped poor Moshe. "But Rabbi, I don't even have one ruble."

"Maybe you could sell something to get the money," replied the Baal Shem Tov.

"But Rabbi, look around. I don't have anything of value to sell," said Reb Moshe.

"Why don't you sell the bedding?" suggested the Baal Shem Tov.

The followers were so embarrassed by this conversation, they couldn't even look in the direction of Reb Moshe or his wife.

Once Reb Moshe realized that the Baal Shem Tov was serious about his request, he asked if he could wait until the next morning for the eighteen rubles.

"Fine, we can wait until tomorrow," answered the Baal Shem Tov, "but then we have to be on our way."

The next morning, Reb Moshe gathered up all the pillows and blankets in the house and took them to the marketplace. A few hours later, he returned with exactly eighteen rubles.

"Here Rabbi," he said, as he hesitantly handed the money to the Baal Shem Tov. With barely a thank you, the Baal Shem Tov took the money. Then he got into the wagon and motioned for the rest to get in also. As the wagon pulled away, the Baal Shem Tov yelled back to Reb Moshe, "G•d be with you."

Moshe, his wife, and the children followed the wagon for a short time, hoping that the Baal Shem Tov would stop and return the eighteen rubles. But the Baal Shem Tov never even looked back. The wagon soon disappeared from sight.

Moshe returned to an empty house, a crying wife, and starving children. By this time, it was late afternoon and time to pray Mincha. He was so upset, he could barely speak. But he prayed as never before. Big tears streamed down his face. He begged G•d to provide him and his family with food, some money, and good health.

That night, the family got into the bed with empty stomachs, and huddled together for warmth. In the middle of the night, Moshe heard a loud knocking at the door. "Who is it?" he asked fearfully.

A rough peasant voice answered, "Moshke, let me in. I'm freezing, and I want a glass of whiskey."

Reb Moshe had sold his last bit of whiskey more than a week earlier. But he was afraid of the peasant, so he opened the door and let him in. He told him to sit down and get warm, while he got him a drink of whiskey. Then, Reb Moshe went into the next room and poured a cup of water into the empty whiskey barrel. He sloshed the water around in the barrel, and then he poured it back into the cup. "Here," he said, handing the full cup to the peasant.

The peasant downed it in one gulp. "Uhmm," he uttered with satisfaction, as he licked his lips. "I really needed a good, strong drink. And what you just served me was really good and very strong. The only problem is that I don't have any money, so I will have to pay you later."

Moshe, still sleepy said, "Sure. Pay me when you can."

He lay down again to sleep, thinking, "What a day. What a night." A few hours later, he was again awakened by a loud knocking at the door.

"Who is it?" he yelled out. It was the same peasant, back for another glass of whiskey. Moshe served him as before, and this time the peasant handed him a dirt-covered coin that he took from his pocket. "Here. I don't know how much it is worth, but it should cover my drinks."

When Reb Moshe took the coin to the market the next day, he learned that the coin was worth enough to pay for much more than the peasant had drunk.

When the peasant returned again the very next night for another glass of whiskey, Moshe gave him a drink and the change from the coin. The peasant was astonished at

Moshe's honesty, and began coming every night. It wasn't long before Moshe had many customers and liquor sales were booming. He was getting richer by the day. Soon, the days of poverty were over, and Moshe became involved in other lucrative businesses.

About one year later, the Baal Shem Tov and the same group of followers happened to be passing by the little village where Reb Moshe lived. Instead of a dilapidated house, there stood a stately mansion surrounded by a number of smaller, but equally beautiful buildings. The followers stared with open mouths. "Rebbe, what happened?" they asked.

"All of this wealth was set aside for Reb Moshe on Rosh Hashanah," explained the Baal Shem Tov. "But he did not receive it, because he accepted his poverty without any complaint. As you know it says in the Tehillim, 'You open Your hand and fulfill the will of every living being.'[3] So I had to take everything he owned from him. When he was left without food and even his bedding, he had no one to turn to but the Holy One, Blessed be He. And from one sincere prayer requesting livelihood, G•d heard. He opened His hand to fulfill the requests of our friend Moshe.

---

3 Psalm 145:16.

So the poor man of last year is a rich man today, thanks to his fervent prayer."

And so it was.

———— • ————

Chapter Ten

TORAH STUDY

The Baal Shem Tov taught that when studying Torah, keep in mind before Whom you stand, for you can be separated from the Creator through improper Torah study.

THE BOOK

When Yisrael ben Eliezer was fourteen years old, he left the holy community of Horodenka, where the local people had cared for him after the death of his parents, Rabbi Eliezer and Rebbetzyn Sarah.

In time, he wandered back to Okup, the village where he was born. It was then that he discovered a yearning in his heart that was only satisfied by the study of the Holy Torah.

Young Yisrael (then known as Yisroelic) was a shamash[1] and lived in the same synagogue. But, he was very

---

[1] Synagogue caretaker.

careful not to show his passion for the Torah to anyone.
By day, he slept on the benches, and everyone thought he
was just an ignorant Jewish boy. But after the last man
closed the holy book he was studying and left the synagogue, Yisroelic stood and studied the Holy Torah all night
by candlelight.

In another city, Rabbi Adam Baal Shem, an elderly holy *Tzaddik* dwelled. Years before, Rabbi Adam had mas-
tered the Torah and the Kaballah, but he was still not
satisfied. He prayed and prayed, "Dearest G•d, I beg of
you to reveal to me the innermost secrets of Your Torah."

One night, Rabbi Adam dreamt that he was in the
Machpelah.[2] There, deep in the underground cave, Rabbi
Adam was given The Book, the Word of the Ever-Present
G•d, and the ability to understand its contents. Until
then, this deepest of all knowledge had been possessed by
only six others: Adam, Abraham, Joseph, Moses, Joshua
ben Nun, and King Solomon.

From that moment on, Rabbi Adam spent all of his
time studying the secret knowledge in The Book. But as
he grew older, he began to wonder to whom he would give
The Book, when his time came. So he prayed, "Dearest
G•d, I must find someone to whom I can pass on this

---

[2] A cave in Hebron where Adam and Eve, Abraham and Sarah, Isaac
and Rebecca, and Yaakov and Leah are buried.

sacred text. Please send me a son to carry on the work." Soon after, he was blessed with a son. As the son grew, he taught him the Torah and the Kaballah. But, Rabbi Adam's son did not have an endless thirst for knowledge; he did not merit receiving The Book.

Not knowing to whom he should pass it on, Rabbi Adam prepared a dream question. "To whom should I give The Book?" he asked each night, just before retiring.

One night the answer came. "Give The Book to Yisrael son of Eliezer, who lives in Okup." When Rabbi Adam awoke, he called his son and gave him The Book. "This book contains the only Torah that I've not studied with you."

"But father," cried his son. "Am I not worthy to learn it?"

"I am sorry my son," Rabbi Adam said gently. "It is not you. It is just not for your soul. Take The Book to Yisrael son of Eliezer, who lives in Okup, because The Book belongs to him. Maybe he will accept you as a student and instruct you in this deepest of all Torah."

Soon thereafter, Rabbi Adam passed onto the next world, and Rabbi Adam's son moved to the town of Okup. The local townspeople were puzzled as to why such a great Torah scholar had come to live in their little town.

He explained, "Friends, my holy father, Rabbi Adam the Tzaddik, told me to find a wife and settle here in Okup."

Upon hearing that, they exclaimed, "Oh Rabbi, we are thrilled to be blessed with you! And as far as a wife, with G•d's Will, it will be arranged soon."

Many marriageable girls were suggested. Rabbi Adam's son married a rich man's daughter and began a routine of studying Torah in the synagogue where Yisrael served as the shamash. All this time, he looked for a deeply spiritual person named Rabbi Yisrael ben Eliezer, but was unable to find him.

Eventually, he noticed the boy called Yisroelic, who took care of the synagogue. One night, while pretending to sleep, Rabbi Adam's son saw Yisroelic study a holy book of Torah by candlelight throughout the entire night.

Early in the morning, when the boy lay down on one of the benches to sleep, Rabbi Adam's son took a page of The Book and carefully placed it on Yisroelic's chest. The boy stirred and picked up the page. As he began to read, he awoke fully. His face turned red and his eyes shone bright. He stood up and became totally engrossed in studying the page.

Within a few minutes Rabbi Adam's son knew that he had found Yisrael ben Eliezer to whom The Book belonged. So he gave him the rest of The Book and explained, "My father, Rabbi Adam the Tzaddik, instructed me to give The Book to you. I beg of you, please take me as your student and teach me the Torah from The Book." Yisrael agreed and they began to study together.

Soon, Rabbi Adam's son asked his father-in-law to hire Yisrael as his helper, and to build him a study house on the outskirts of the village, so that he could study without any disruption. His father-in-law agreed. The two of them poured over The Book in the little study house, devoting themselves to it. They soared through the hidden worlds, exploring the source of the Torah.

In time, Yisrael noticed that Rabbi Adam's son had become thinner and weaker. He asked him what was the problem, but Rabbi Adam's son did not respond. Yisrael was worried about the health of his friend, and he persisted with his questions. Finally Rabbi Adam's son replied. "Yisrael, the more I learn, the greater the emptiness I feel. I need to know the *Ineffable Name*.[3] Otherwise, I just cannot go on."

Yisrael nodded with understanding but said, "My dearest friend. We are not pure enough. We just cannot go that far." Rabbi Adam's son no longer asked to know the Name. Yet he continued to weaken.

---

[3] 72 letter name of G•d.

In desperation, Yisrael decided to try and learn the Ineffable Name — before his friend simply left the body. "All right. We will try. May G•d save us."

So they fasted from one Shabbos to another. On Friday afternoon, just before the second Shabbos, they went to the Mikveh to purify themselves. After reciting the Shabbos evening prayers, they concentrated on a certain combination of Hebrew letters and entered into a deep trance. Yisrael prayed, "Dearest G•d, please reveal to us your ineffable Name!"

Suddenly, they were both jolted back into everyday consciousness. With great concern, Yisrael said to Rabbi Adam's son, "Oh my G•d! We lost our concentration and the *Prince of Fire*[4] is descending to take us. We only have one hope. We must stay awake all night and study The Book without letting our eyes close with sleep for even a second!"

Rabbi Adam's son looked at Yisrael with fear in his eyes.

Yisrael put his hand on his shoulder and said, "Don't worry, I will help you."

And so Yisrael and Rabbi Adam's son stood next to each other and read out loud from The Book. But just before morning, Rabbi Adam's son could not keep his

---

[4]Angel Gabriel.

eyes open any longer. He fell into a deep sleep from which he never awoke.

And so it was.

———— • ————

Chapter Eleven

TEACHER

The Baal Shem Tov said, "There are two levels in the study of Torah: Torah of the mind and Torah of the heart. The mind ponders, comprehends, and understands; the heart feels. I have come to reveal Torah as it effects the heart as well."

TEACHING KABBALAH

Once there was the time, when the *talmid chacham*,[1] Reb Dov Ber was in a period of spiritual retreat and concealed his great knowledge of all levels of Torah. He worked as a *melamed*[2] in a small village near Lvov where Rabbi Yaakov Yehoshua Falk Katz (the author of *Pnei Yehoshua*) was the Rabbi. At least once a week, Reb Dov Ber went to Lvov to study Torah with the Rabbi.

When Reb Yaakov left Lvov to take a position as a rabbi in a distant city, his son-in-law took over as the new

---

[1] A scholar of Talmud.
[2] Teacher of young boys.

Lvov Rabbi. Before Rabbi Yaakov's departure, his son-in-law confided in him of his concern about ruling on questions of Jewish law. Reb Yaakov put his arm around him and said, "Do not worry. If you have a difficult question, ask Reb Berel." Reb Berel was Reb Yaakov's nickname for Dov Ber.

As for Reb Dov Ber, he continued to visit Lvov, and now studied with the son-in-law. And as Rabbi Yaakov Yehoshua had suggested, the new rabbi always asked Reb Dov Ber's advice, when he had to rule on thorny questions of Jewish law.

As the two men studied the holy books together, they formed a close friendship. This friendship continued throughout their lives, even after Reb Dov Ber become famous and known as the Mezritcher Maggid (the successor to the Baal Shem Tov).

Following Reb Dov Ber's return from his spiritual exile, he began to suffer from a problem with his legs. He only had a little strength in his legs, and they continued to weaken. Moreover, he suffered increasing pain. Although he sought help from many doctors, and tried various folk remedies, nothing helped. Reb Dov Ber was forced to walk with crutches.

Many of his friends and colleagues suggested that he go to the Baal Shem Tov, who was already famous as a miracle worker and healer. Even his old friend, the Rabbi of Lvov (the Pnei Yehoshua), came to Reb Dov Ber and urged him to ask the Baal Shem Tov for a blessing that his legs would heal.

But Reb Dov Ber refused, saying, "It is forbidden to seek the help of one who uses practical Kabbalah to heal the sick. And even if the rabbis permitted it, I would not go. I have a hundred questions about the practice and teachings of the Baal Shem Tov and I will not go before my questions are answered!"

With the passage of time, however, Reb Dov Ber's pain and suffering increased. Finally, he decided to travel to the holy community of Mezibush, where the Baal Shem Tov lived, and seek his help. By that time, he had heard so many reports of the Baal Shem Tov's piety and of his prophetic powers that he wanted to see for himself if the stories were true.

The trip to Mezibush took two full days by horse and wagon. By the time Reb Dov Ber reached the Baal Shem Tov's Shule, he was angry with himself for losing so much time from his holy studies. But soon after his arrival, he had Yichidus with the Baal Shem Tov.

Reb Dov Ber had heard so much about the spiritual qualities of the Baal Shem Tov, he expected him to expound upon mystical teachings from the Torah. But to

his chagrin and surprise, during their first meeting, the
Baal Shem Tov did not discuss Torah at all. Instead, he
told a seemingly immaterial story about a nondescript
wagon trip he had taken with Alexei, his wagon driver.
Reb Dov Ber left the meeting disappointed, but decided he
would see the Baal Shem Tov one more time, in the hopes
of seeing for himself what had made the Baal Shem Tov
so famous.

The very next day, the Baal Shem Tov invited Dov Ber
to meet with him again. During their time together, the
Baal Shem Tov told Dov Ber several more seemingly
irrelevant stories, similar to the one he had told the day
before. As soon as the Baal Shem Tov had finished speaking, Reb Dov Ber got up and left.

As he walked out the door of the Baal Shem Tov's
study, he shook his head in disbelief. "How could I have
been so naïve as to listen to — and actually believe — all
of those stories about this man?" He clapped his hand to
his forehead. "And look how many days I have taken from
studying Talmud for this nonsense!"

At that moment, he gave up the idea of learning anything from the Baal Shem Tov. He resolved to return
home to his studies as soon as possible. He went directly
to the inn where he was lodging, and told his wagon
driver to prepare the horse and wagon for the return trip.

Just as Reb Dov Ber was getting into the wagon to leave Mezibush, a messenger handed him a sealed envelope from the Baal Shem Tov. He opened the envelope and read:

> *"Dear Reb Dov Ber,*
>
> *Please meet with me again in my study at your earliest convenience.*
>
> *Rabbi Yisrael Baal Shem Tov."*

Reb Dov Ber got out of the wagon. Shaking his head in bewilderment, he trudged off to the house of the Baal Shem Tov, "for one last meeting."

When he entered the study, the Baal Shem Tov was sitting behind his desk deeply engrossed in a holy book. Rabbi Yisrael looked up and gestured to Reb Dov Ber to sit down. After a few minutes of silence, the Baal Shem Tov asked, "Dov Ber, do you understand Kabbalah?"

"Yes," Dov Ber answered, surprised.

With that, the Baal Shem Tov opened the *Etz Chaim*,[3] and pointed to a particular passage. "Good," he said. "Now can you explain this passage to me?"

---

[3] A fundamental book of Kabbalah.

Reb Dov Ber took the Sefer from the Baal Shem Tov. He read the passage to himself and began to explain it.

When he had finished, the Baal Shem Tov prodded, "Could you give me a deeper explanation of that passage?"

Reb Dov Ber began again and gave a deeper explanation.

"Very insightful, Reb Dov Ber," responded the Baal Shem Tov, with a slight nod. "But what about an even deeper explanation?"

Undaunted, Reb Dov Ber gave a still deeper explanation.

"Still, there is a much better explanation," said the Baal Shem Tov.

Reb Dov Ber responded with annoyance, "If you have a better explanation, I want to hear it."

"Then please stand," Rabbi Yisrael uttered. Dov Ber took his crutches and stood with some difficulty. The Baal Shem Tov began to analyze the same Kabbalistic passage. The passage included the names of several Heavenly angels, and as he spoke, the room filled with a brilliant light. Reb Dov Ber could *see* the Heavenly angels as they were named. When the Baal Shem Tov finished, he looked into the eyes of Reb Dov Ber and said, "Your explanations are correct, but there is more to learn."

Reb Dov Ber was overwhelmed. He decided at that moment to remain in Mezibush and study Torah from his new Rebbe, the Baal Shem Tov.

Soon thereafter he joined the Chevrayah Kadisha, the Baal Shem Tov's inner circle. In fact, he was such an important and gifted student, that he later became the Baal Shem Tov's successor as the leader of the fledgling Chassidic movement.

When the Rabbi of Lvov learned that his old friend Reb Dov Ber had become a close follower of the Baal Shem Tov, he decided to pay him a visit. While they were talking, he gently chided Reb Dov Ber, "And what about these hundred questions you once had about the Baal Shem Tov?"

"I will tell you what happened that answered all my hundred questions at one time." Reb Dov Ber went on to tell the story about his first visit. "I stood up while the Rebbe explained a passage from the Sefer Etz Chaim. The Rebbe's eyes were glowing. The very angels mentioned in the passage were visible. I kept asking myself if the man was truly human. How could a man born of woman achieve such holy power? Had he perhaps fallen from Heaven? The vision he showed me was enough to remove all my doubts. Humans can have doubts about other human beings, but how can one question such a G•dly creature?"

And so it was.

———— • ————

Chapter Twelve

STORY TELLING

The Baal Shem Tov said that each person should tell a friend the story of the deeds of a Tzaddik.

THE STORY TELLER

And then there was the time, shortly before his leaving this world, that the holy Baal Shem Tov called for his closest disciples, and instructed them what to do next. The last disciple with whom he spoke was Reb Yaakov. He whispered to him, "Reb Yaakov. After my death, travel from town to town, and wherever you go, repeat my Torah, and tell what I did during my life."

Yaakov was perplexed. "Rebbe, why have you burdened me with a life of wandering and poverty?"

The Baal Shem Tov responded, "My dear Reb Yaakov. You will not live a life of wandering and poverty. In fact, you will be highly rewarded for doing what I ask of you.

And when the time comes for your wandering to end, a sign will be given to you."

Shortly after the Baal Shem Tov left this world, each of his disciples began his assigned task. Reb Yaakov slipped into his backpack, took his walking stick, and began to travel from town to town. He repeatedly said to himself, "Dear L•rd, what in the world am I getting myself into?" His question was soon to be answered.

He discovered that he was warmly welcomed at every inn and Shule, wherever he traveled. People eagerly gathered to hear his inspiring stories of the Baal Shem Tov. And since he had been a member of the Chevrayah Kadisha, the inner circle, he knew thousands of stories. At the inns, he was given food and lodging. At the Shules, he received money that had been collected just for him. Although he did live a life of travel, as the Baal Shem Tov had predicted, he did not live a life of poverty.

After several years of traveling from town to town, Reb Yaakov heard about an Italian nobleman who loved stories of the Baal Shem Tov. The rumor was that he gave a gold coin for every Baal Shem Tov story that was told him.

"I will go and tell him all the stories I know," thought Yaakov, "and then I will be a wealthy man."

So Yaakov set out for Rome. As he traveled, he reviewed in his mind all of the stories he knew about the Baal Shem Tov, as well as the teachings he had heard directly from the holy mouth of his Rebbe.

When he arrived in Rome, he inquired after the nobleman. Sure enough, he was directed to the imposing residence of a Baron and his many servants. When the master of the house learned that a Reb Yaakov had come with stories of the Baal Shem Tov, he warmly welcomed him.

"Tomorrow, when we are sitting around the Shabbos table, you can tell us your stories," said the Baron. Yaakov wondered why so rich a man as the Baron wanted to hear stories of Rabbi Yisrael.

When the time came for the evening Shabbos meal, Yaakov was seated next to the Baron at a large table, around which were seated many other guests. Everyone anticipated that Reb Yaakov would know many stories about the Rebbe, since he had been one of his close followers.

After Kiddush over the wine and HaMotzi, the Baron asked Yaakov whether he had ever met the Baal Shem Tov in person.

"I saw him every day," answered Yaakov. "He was my teacher."

"Tell me," said the Baron. "What did the Rebbe look like?"

Yaakov tried to picture the Baal Shem Tov in his mind, but he could not conjure up a clear image of him. He answered, "Like no other man," and then fell quiet.

When the evening Shabbos meal had ended, the Baron said, "Reb Yaakov, please honor us with a story."

Yaakov wanted to speak, but he could not think of a single thing to say. He could not remember anything about the Baal Shem Tov. Yaakov looked about the table, and saw that everyone was looking at him. Finally he said, "I cannot speak right now."

"Never mind. It is late," said the Baron. "Tomorrow, during the second meal of Shabbos, you will tell us a few stories."

But, at the second meal, and even later, after Havdalah, Reb Yaakov was still unable to remember any stories about the Baal Shem Tov. He was deeply embarrassed and could not understand his loss of memory. He could only keep thinking that as soon as Shabbos was over, he would leave.

But at the conclusion of Shabbos, the Baron kindly said, "Reb Yaakov, please stay another day. Perhaps you will remember something." Yaakov did not want to stay any longer. But he was without funds and far from home. So he agreed to stay.

He wandered by himself in the garden the next day, but nothing came into his mind. The Baron urged him to stay longer, in any case. And although he was very embarrassed, Reb Yaakov remained several more days. Finally, he could not stand the humiliation any longer and told the Baron, "I must go."

The Baron gave him a small bag of gold coins, and said, "Reb Yaakov, take this. And if you do remember anything about the Baal Shem Tov, please return."

Then, the Baron put Reb Yaakov into his own carriage, and instructed his driver to take him as far as he wanted to go.

When the carriage had traveled just out of view of the Baron's palatial estate, a story jumped into Reb Yaakov's mind. He shouted to the driver, "Turn the carriage around. Return to the Baron! I just remembered a story!" The driver turned the carriage around. The Baron came running to meet them, when he saw the coach with Reb Yaakov coming up the drive.

Yaakov walked with the Baron from the carriage to the house. He started to speak, so afraid was he that he might forget again. "It is very strange," he said. "The only story I remember is one that I have never thought about since the events occurred. And this is one story that I am sure you have never heard from anyone else."

THE STORY TOLD BY REB YAAKOV

"**Once**, during the week of Passover, the Baal Shem Tov asked me whether I wanted to accompany him and several other disciples on a long journey. Of course, I wanted to go.

"For our travels, we each took with us a small bag with Tallis and Teffilin, as well as some food and a little *mash-ka*.[1] We got into the Rebbe's wagon, which, as you have probably heard many times before, was driven by the Rebbe's driver, Alexei.

"As usual, after we left town, Alexei had a few l'chaims — you know, a little schnapps — and fell asleep. The horses drew the wagon along without being guided by a human hand. We rode all night and covered a great distance, as was often the case when we traveled with the Master.

"By morning, we came to a large, foreign city unknown to us. The streets were filled with people dressed for a holiday. We continued on until we reached the Jewish ghetto. There, no one could be seen on the streets. The

---

[1] Liquor.

doors of all of the houses were closed shut, and every window was shuttered.

"The horses stopped before one of the houses. Rabbi Yisrael went to the door and knocked. When no one answered, he knocked again more loudly.

Finally, he yelled, 'Open up, in the name of G•d.'

"Then, from behind the door we heard the voice of what sounded like an elderly woman. 'Who is it?' she cried.

"'It is Rabbi Yisrael Ben Eliezer,' said the Baal Shem Tov. The door was unlocked and opened a crack. It was obvious to the woman that we were Jews, and we were let into the house. The door was quickly closed and locked again.

"The old woman cried, 'Rabbi, do you want to be killed? Today is Easter. Every year in this city on Easter, a Jew is taken and burned alive. If a Jew is found walking in the streets, or if a Jew even shows himself or herself in the window, he or she is taken and burned on the cross in the town square. If no Jew is seen, one is chosen by lot.'

"The Baal Shem Tov attempted to reassure her. 'Don't be afraid. Let me do as I must.' Then Rabbi Yisrael went to a window overlooking the town square. He pulled back the curtains and opened the shutters. He stood by the window and watched what was taking place in the town square.

"A large altar was being built in the square. Next to it was a wooden cross, with logs piled around the base. Here, some hapless Jew would be tied to the cross and set afire. As we watched, a large and noisy crowd of people thronged into the square. Besides the common people dressed in their holiday clothes, there were priests in their robes. Among them was one priest dressed in the robes of a higher office, who stood on the altar.

"The Baal Shem Tov pointed to that priest and said to me, 'That man is the Bishop. Go down and tell him that Rabbi Yisrael is waiting for him in this house.'

"I went to the door. The woman screamed, 'Don't go! They will drag you to their altar and burn you alive!' But since the Baal Shem Tov had instructed me, I went.

"I took a deep breath, opened the door, and went outside. No one seemed to notice me as I walked through the crowd. I came to the foot of the altar and called out to the Bishop, 'Bishop, I have a message for you.'

"He said, 'Come up and tell it to me.'

"I went up onto the platform and whispered in the Bishop's ear, 'Rabbi Yisrael Ben Eliezer wants you to come to him at once.'

"The Bishop was startled. He said to me, 'Go back and tell the Rabbi that I will come in a few hours.'

"I went down from the altar and walked through the crowd, and again no one seemed to notice my presence. Rabbi Yisrael stood waiting for me at the door of the house. When I told him what the Bishop had said, he was insistent. 'Go back and tell him he must come to me at once.'

"The other people in the house, who by now had come downstairs to see with whom the old woman was speaking, cried out, 'Don't go! They are about to begin the service. They will burn you alive!'

"Nevertheless, I followed my Rebbe's instructions, and returned through the crowd of people to the altar. The Bishop was now already conducting the service. He was speaking loudly to the crowd.

"When I had gotten to the foot of the altar, he looked down at me. I yelled up to him, 'Rabbi Yisrael Ben Eliezer wants to speak with you, Now!'

He yielded and said, 'I will come with you.' Then, to the crowd of people he said, 'The service is over for now. I will return later to speak.' We walked quickly to the house. Rabbi Yisrael was waiting at the door.

"Rabbi Yisrael escorted the Bishop into another room and closed the door. Several hours passed. Then Rabbi Yisrael came out of the room alone, and said to me, 'We are ready to leave.' We got into our wagon and began the trip home to Mezibush. And that is as much as I know of the story," concluded Reb Yaakov.

The Baron looked directly at Yaakov and said, "Don't you recognize me?"

"Oh my G•d! How can it be? You are the Bishop!" gasped Yaakov.

The Baron put his arm around Yaakov and said, "You have just saved my soul!"

After they had spoken for a while, Reb Yaakov asked, "What did happen in that room? I have always wondered what the Baal Shem Tov said to you."

The Baron replied, "When I entered the room, the Baal Shem Tov said, 'Moshe are you ready to return to the path of your forefathers and live as a Jew?' I started to cry, and the black cloud covering my soul suddenly lifted.

"I am descended from a long line of learned and holy rabbis. But when I was still a young student, my yetzer hora[2] overwhelmed me. I converted to Christianity and became a priest. The Christians were very pleased that I had converted. I quickly advanced to higher and higher positions in the Church. As I gained greater stature, I became increasingly cruel to other Jews. And the crueler I became, the more I advanced. Finally, I was made Bishop

---

[2] Evil Inclination.

over that city. And every Easter, I burned a Jew on the cross.

"One night, I had a vivid dream: A group of holy rabbis stood around a long table. And on that table was my blackened soul, awaiting judgment. At one end of the table was a very holy Tzaddik. Suddenly, I realized that these rabbis were my ancestors. The rabbis all agreed that my soul was doomed, because the yetzer hora had utterly destroyed the good spirit within it.

"Then the Tzaddik said, 'If he repents, the Gates of Heaven are not closed to him.' The Tzaddik touched me with his hand, and my soul became filled with light. And then I heard my ancestors call the Tzaddik. His name was Rabbi Yisrael Ben Eliezer.

"Then came that day when you saw me in the town square. Because of my dream, I did not want to go through with the killing. But everybody was praising me in the expectation of the auto-da-fé. I thought to myself, 'This is the last time.'

"But then you came, and said you were sent by Rabbi Yisrael Ben Eliezer. I knew that my time had come. Still, I wanted to finish the service and hear the cheering of the people one more time. So then I said to you that I would come in a few hours. But when the Baal Shem Tov sent

you a second time, I knew that I had to go at once. And so
I went."

"He instructed me that I must sell all of my posses-
sions. I was to divide the money I received into three
parts. He said to me, 'With one part, buy your freedom
from the Church. Give the second part to the poor. And
use the third part to go to a distant country, do good
deeds, repent, and live your life as a Jew. Because of the
holiness of your forefathers, there is still hope that you
will be pardoned for your sins.' "

"'But how will I know that I have been pardoned by
G•d?' I asked.

Rabbi Yisrael said to me, 'When a man comes to you
and tells you your own story, then you will know that
your sins have been pardoned.'"

"When you came," said the Baron to Yaakov, "I recog-
nized you at once. But when you could not remember
anything, I realized that I had not yet been pardoned. So I
began to do deeper repentance. Then, when you started to
go away, I thought, 'I am lost.' But I know that Rabbi
Yisrael Ben Eliezer interceded for me again in Heaven.
Thank G•d I am saved."

Then, the Baron gave Yaakov half of his fortune. And
Yaakov knew that the sign was given to him, and his days
of wandering were over. But he never stopped his telling

of the stories of the Baal Shem Tov, who was a great light for the Jewish people during his life and even after his passing to the next world.

And so it was.

——— • ———

APPENDIX

Below is a free translation of the letter (called the Epistle) that Rabbi Yisrael Baal Shem Tov wrote to his brother-in-law, Rabbi Gershon of Kitov, who was then living in the Holy Land. In the letter, the Baal Shem Tov describes his encounter with the Moshiach and what the latter said regarding the Baal Shem Tov's central role in causing the Moshiach to emerge in this world as the King of the Jewish Nation in the land of Israel. The Baal Shem Tov gave the letter to one of his closest followers, Rabbi Yaakov Yosef of Polonoye, to deliver to his brother-in-law, Rabbi Gershon. But because of circumstances, R. Yaakov Yosef did not travel to the Land of Israel, and the letter remained in his hands so as to benefit the Children of Israel. This is one of the only writings believed to have actually been written by the Baal Shem Tov. The following is the Koretz version and it has been adapted to make it more readable.

THE EPISTLE

To my beloved brother-in-law, and my friend who is as dear to me as my own soul and heart, who is the distinguished rabbinic scholar, the Chassid, famous in the study of Torah and in his piety, his honor, our teacher, Rabbi Avraham Gershon, may his lamp shine, and peace be to all that is his. And to his modest wife Bluma and all her children, may they all be granted the blessing of life, Amen selah!

I received your holy letter, which you sent by the emissary from Jerusalem, at the fair in Loka in 5510 [1750]. It was written with extreme brevity. In it you said that you had already written at great length and sent the letters with someone who traveled by way of Egypt. However, those letters which were written at length did not reach me, and it caused me great anguish not to see what you wrote in detail with your holy handwriting.

Certainly this is because of the worsening conditions here and in nearby countries. Because of our many sins, the plague has spread to every country. It has even come close to here, in the holy community of Mohilov, and the districts of Walachia and Kedar.

Also, in your letter you said that those new interpretations and secrets which I wrote to you, through the scribe, the rabbi and preacher of the holy community of Polonnoye, did not reach you. This too caused me great pain because you would have certainly derived great satisfaction from them. However, I have now forgotten certain parts of what I wrote. So I'm writing to you here, in brief, some details of what I remember.

On Rosh HaShanah of the Hebrew year 5507 (1747), I made an Aliyat HaNeshama (Ascent of the Soul) using the oath that you know. I saw amazing things in a vision, which I had not seen since I acquired my level of understanding. It would be impossible to tell you, even face to face, what I saw and learned during that ascent.

When I returned to the lower *Gan Eden*,[1] I saw the souls of the living and dead, some known to me and others unknown to me. They were without limit and number and they were running and returning by rising from world to world through the "column" which is known to those initiated into the Kabbalah. They expressed such great and extensive joy, that the mouth is not able to express it and the physical ear is unable to hear it. Also, there were present many wicked people who had repented, and their sins were forgiven.

---

[1] Spiritual Garden of Eden.

It was a time of great acceptance, and even to me, it was exceedingly amazing that so many were accepted by G•d in their repentance — some of them you too know. There was amongst them, also, very great joy, and they too rose up in the above-mentioned ascents. And they all begged me and pleaded with me to ascend together with them and be their helper and provider. They said "Your exalted Torah Eminence, the L•rd has granted you a special understanding to perceive and know these mat-ters." Because of the great joy which I saw amongst them, I decided to ascend with them.

And I saw in a vision that Samael had risen to accuse with great delight as never before. He issued decrees of forced conversion against a number of souls who would then be killed by unnatural deaths.

I was horrified and I actually risked my life to save them. I asked my Master and teacher[2] to go with me, for it is exceedingly dangerous to ascend to the upper worlds and since I arrived at my present level, I had not risen in such ascents.

I went up, level after level, until I entered the palace of the Moshiach, where the Moshiach studies Torah with all the Tannaim and the Righteous Ones, and with the Seven

---

2 Achiyah HaShiloni

Shepherds. I beheld very great joy there, but I did not know the reason for this extreme happiness.

I thought this joy was, G•d forbid, because of my demise from this world. But they told me later that I was not deceased and that they derived tremendous pleasure when I performed *Yichudim*[3] in the world by means of the holy Torah. But as to the meaning of this great rejoicing, I still do not know.

And I asked the Moshiach, "When are you coming, my Master?"

He answered me, **"By this you shall know it: Once your teachings become publicly known and revealed throughout the world; and when your wellsprings have overflowed beyond, imparting to others what I have taught you and you have grasped; so that they too will be able to perform Yichudim and Ascents of the Soul as you do. Then all the kelipot will perish; and it will be a time of favor and salvation."**

I was bewildered at this response. I felt great anguish because of the length of time the Moshiach implied it would take until he came.

However while I was there, I learned three *Segulos*[4] and three Holy Names which were easy to learn and to

---

[3] Contemplative unifications
[4] Charm or remedy of spiritual potency.

explain to others. So I felt reassured, and I thought that perhaps, using these Segulos and Holy Names, my *Chaburah*,[5] might also be able to attain my spiritual level. That is, they would be able to practice Ascents of the Soul, and learn and understand the Supernal Mysteries as I do.

But I was not granted permission to reveal them during my life, and further, I am under oath behalf to teach them to you. But I was not permitted and I am under oath not to do this.

But this I can tell you. May the Blessed L•rd help you and may your paths be in G•d's presence and do not depart from them, especially in the Holy Land. While you are praying or studying, with every utterance and all that comes from your lips, intend to unify it with a Name of G•d because in every single letter there are Worlds and Souls and Divinity. And these letters rise and bind and unite with each other and in a true unity with G•dliness to form a word. And include your Soul with them in every level of the above. Then all the worlds will unite as one and rise up and make unaccountable joy and pleasure without limit.

If you can imagine the joy of the bride and groom, in its smallness and materiality, you can imagine how much

---

[5] Inner circle of followers.

more is the joy in the Upper World. Certainly the L•rd will "be thy help," and wherever you turn, you will prosper and succeed. As it says, "Give to a wise man, and he will be yet wiser!" (Proverbs 9:9). Also, pray for me with the intention in your mind that I be privileged to share in the inheritance of the L•rd (1 Samuel 26:19) while I'm still alive; and also pray for the remnant of Israel that is outside the Land of Israel.

And I also asked there: "Why has the L•rd done this; What does the heat of this great anger mean that so many Jewish souls were given over to Samael to be killed — and of them, a number who were baptized and then killed?" They gave me permission to ask Samael himself.

And so I asked Samael: "What is the point of this and what do you think of them converting and then being killed?" He answered me, "My intention is for the sake of Heaven. And so it happened afterward, because of our many sins, that in the holy community of Zaslav there was a *blood libel*⁶ against several souls. Two of them converted and were later killed, and the rest sanctified the Name of Heaven with great sanctity and died unnatural deaths. Then there were blood libels in the holy communities of Sibatuvka and Dunawitz, and there no one

---

⁶ Claiming that the Jews put Christian blood in the Matzahs (unleavened bread) eaten during Passover.

converted after they had seen what happened in Zaslav. Rather, all of them gave over their lives for the sanctification of G•d. They sanctified the Name of Heaven and withstood the test. In the merit of this martyrdom, may our Moshiach come and take his vengeance and redeem his land and his people.

And on Rosh Hashanah of 5510 [1749], I performed an Ascent of the Soul using the oath you know, and I saw a great accusation against Israel, in which Samael was almost given permission to destroy entire countries and communities. I risked my life and prayed, "Let us fall by the Hand of the L•rd, and not by the hand of man." And they granted me permission to have the anti-Semitic persecutions exchanged for a great pestilence against animals and a plague against people the likes of which had not previously occurred in all the lands of Poland and other nearby countries. And that is exactly what happened. The pestilence spread to such an extent that it cannot be related. And the plague too spread in other countries.

After a long and engaged discussion as to what to do with my Chaburah, we decided to recite the *Ketores*[7] in the morning prayers in order to nullify the judgments

[7] Torah liturgy in the Siddur about incense (Ketores) used in the Bais HaMikdash (Holy Temple).

mentioned above. Then it was revealed to me in a night vision, "But did not you yourself choose the plague, by saying, 'Let us fall by the hand of the L•rd,'" as mentioned above. "Why then do you wish to nullify the decree of plague now? Surely an accuser can not become a defender!

From then on I did not recite Ketores, and I did not pray about this. But on Hoshanah Rabbah, I went to the synagogue with the entire community, and I tried to intercede on behalf of Israel by means of several oaths because of my great fear for the safety of the Jewish community. I recited Ketores once so that the plague would not spread to our vicinity and we were successful with the help of the L•rd.

I wanted to elaborate more and describe what happened at length, but because of my tears when I recall your departure from me, I am not able to speak. But I do ask you to review all my words of admonition which I told you several times. Let them always be in your thoughts, to meditate on them and ponder them thoroughly. Surely you will find in every word all kinds of sweetness, for what I told you is no vain thing. For the L•rd knows that I have not given up on journeying to the Land of Israel, if that be the Will of the L•rd, to be together with you.

But as of now, the time is not right for it.

Also, do not be too upset with me that I have not sent you money, for it is because of the desperate times we have had here with the plague and the famine. The young children of my family, as well as other poor Jews, are dependent upon me to support them and feed them. Our money is all spent . . . there is nothing left but our bodies! But the L•rd willing, when the L•rd shall enlarge . . . then certainly I'll send you money.

Also, my grandson, the young Choson, the honorable Ephraim, is a great Torah prodigy.

Surely if the time is right for it, how fitting it would be for you to come here so that we may see each other face to face and to rejoice in our happiness, as you promised me.

I also ask of you on behalf of the renowned rabbi, the Chassid, our master Yosef Katz, a servant of the L•rd. Please befriend him and offer him all kinds of assistance for "all his deeds are for the sake of Heaven" and are welcome before the blessed L•rd. I also request of you to write on his behalf to the wealthy people to provide adequate support for him, for certainly he will be a source of satisfaction to you if he will be there with you.

Such are the words of your brother-in-law who looks forward to seeing you face to face and prays for a long life for you and your wife and your children, and seeks after your welfare daily and at night as well as for a good long life. Amen, Selah.

Yisrael Besht of the holy community of Mezibush

———— • ————

GLOSSARY

Aliyat HaNeshama — Ascent of the Soul.

Baal Shem — Rabbi that utilized the powers of Kabbalah to heal the sick, ward off demonic spirits and predict the future.

Baal Teshuvah — One who repents and returns to belief in G•d and the observance of the Mitzvos.

Bat Mitzvah — Jewish girl is responsible for her actions at 12 years old.

Benching — Saying the Grace after meals.

Besht — Acronym for Baal Shem Tov.

Challah — Braided bread eaten on Shabbos and festivals.

Chosson — The groom.

Chasana — A wedding.

Chazzan — Leader of communal prayer.

Cheder — Hebrew day school for young boys.

Chaburah — Group of friends.

Chevrayah Kaddisha — Group of Holy friends.

Chuppah — A wedding canopy.

Davened — Praying.

Dveikus — Cleaving to G•d.

Eliyahu HaNavi — Elijah the Prophet.

Festivals — Rosh HaShanah, Yom Kippur, Succos, Pesach, etc.

Gartle — A prayer belt worn by Chassidim.

Ha Kodosh Boruch Hu — The Holy One Blessed be He.

HaMotzi — Blessing said over bread.

Havdalah — a ritual prayer recited at the close of Sabbath and other holy days that marks the separation between holy days and the ordinary days of the week.

Ineffable Name — 72 letter name of G•d.

Kabbalah — The teachings and doctrines that deal with the Jewish Mystical Tradition.

Kallah — The bride.

Kelipot — "Husk" in Kabbalistic thought, the aspect of evil or impurity that obscures the holy and good.

Kiddush — The ritual of sanctification of Shabbos or Yom Tov, usually recited over a cup of wine.

Kvittel — A note in which the petitioner writes out his or her request.

Maariv — The evening prayer service.

Machpelah — A cave in Hebron where Adam and Eve, Abraham and Sarah, Isaac and Rebecca, and Yaakov and Leah are buried.

Mashka — Liquor.

Melavah Malkah — Meal eaten after the conclusion of the Sabbath that celebrates the return of the Shabbos Queen to heaven, where She dwells until the next Sabbath, when She returns once again.

Melamed — Hebrew teacher of young boys.

Mincha — The afternoon prayer service.

Minyan — Ten Jewish men needed for communal prayer.

Mitzvos — Divine commandments.

Mikveh — Pool for ritual immersion.

Mitzvah — Divine commandment.

Moshiach — Messiah.

Niggun — Spritual melody without words.

Parnassah — Monetary livelihood.

Rebbe — Spiritual master and leader of a Chassidic Sect.

Samael — The Chief of the demons.

Satan — Angel that serves as the Adversary.

Sefer — Sacred Hebrew Book.

Segulah — Charm or remedy of mystical potency.

Seudah Shlishit — The third meal, traditionally eaten on Shabbos before sunset.

Shabbos — Sabbath.

Shalom Aleichem — Peace be to you.

Shamash — Synagogue caretaker.

Shule — Synagogue.

Shochet — Ritual slaughterer.

Siddur — The book of daily ritual Hebrew prayers.

Tallis — Prayer shawl.

Tannaim — Jewish Sages of the Mishnah 10 CE — 220CE.

Teffilin — Ritual leather boxes containing verses of the Torah written on parchment, strapped to head and arm while praying.

Tehhilim — Psalms.

Teshuvah — Repentance; literally turning (back to G•d).

Tish — A communal dinner.

Torah —Twenty four canonized scriptures of traditional Judaism. It consists of the Five Books of Moses, the Prophets, and the Writings. The Torah can also mean any spiritual text book or idea that is connected to traditional Judaism.

Tzaddik — Righteous or holy man.

Tzedaka — Charity.

Yetzer Hara — Evil Inclination.

Yichudim — Kabbalistic meditation that unites the Holy
One blessed be He.

Yichidus — Private audience with a Rebbe.

BIBLIOGRAPHY

1. IN PRAISE OF THE BAAL SHEM TOV
   Translated and edited by Dan Ben-Amos and Jerome
   R.Mintz

2. STORIES OF THE BAAL SHEM TOV
   by Rabbi Yisroel Yaakov Klapholtz

3. A TREASURY OF CHASSIDIC TALES ON THE
   FESTIVALS
   by Rabbi Shlomo Yosef Zevin

4. A TREASURY OF CHASSIDIC TALES ON THE TORAH
   by Rabbi Shlomo Yosef Zevin

5. SEEKER OF SLUMBERING SOULS
   by Rabbi Zalman Ruderman

6. THE PATH OF THE BAAL SHEM TOV
   by Rabbi David Sears

7. ESSENTIAL PAPERS ON CHASSIDISM
   Edited by Gershon David Hundert

8.   MEETINGS WITH REMARKABLE SOULS
     by Rabbi Eliahu Klein

9.   CLASSIC CHASSIDIC TALES
     by Meyer Levin

10. Story Telling and Spirituality in Judaism
     by Maggid Yitzhak Buxbaum

11. THE LIGHT BEYOND
     by Rabbi Aryeh Kaplan

12. TZAVA'AT HARIVASH
     by Rabbi Jacob Immanuel Schochet

13. THE LIGHT AND FIRE OF THE BAAL SHEM TOV
     by Maggid Yitzhak Buxbaum

14. THE BESHT
     by Professor Emanuel Etkes

15. Extraordinary Chassidic Tales
     by Rabbi Rafael Nachman Kahn

16. The Great Mission
     by Rabbi Eli Friedman

17. Chassidic Masters
    by Rabbi Aryeh Kaplan

18. The Religious Thought of Chassidim
    by Rabbi Norman Lamm

19. Hasidic Tales
    by Rabbi Rami Shapiro

SOURCES OF THE
BAAL SHEM TOV STORIES

Chapter One

PERFECT FAITH

Sɪᴘᴜʀɪᴍ Uᴍᴀᴍᴏʀɪᴍ Yᴇᴋᴏʀɪᴍ and translated in Sᴛᴏʀɪᴇs ᴏғ ᴛʜᴇ Bᴀᴀʟ Sʜᴇᴍ Tᴏᴠ by Rabbi Y.Y.Klapholtz.

Chapter Two

THE MEANING OF HOSPITALITY

Sʜɪᴠᴄʜᴇɪ HᴀBᴇsʜᴛ and translated in Iɴ Pʀᴀɪsᴇ ᴏғ ᴛʜᴇ Bᴀᴀʟ Sʜᴇᴍ Tᴏᴠ by Mintz and Ben Amos.
Sᴇᴇᴋᴇʀs Oғ Sʟᴜᴍʙᴇʀɪɴɢ Sᴏᴜʟs by Rabbi Moshe Rabin.
Tʜᴇ Lɪɢʜᴛ ᴀɴᴅ Fɪʀᴇ ᴏғ ᴛʜᴇ Bᴀᴀʟ Sʜᴇᴍ Tᴏᴠ by Yitzhak Buxbaum.

Chapter Three

THE WAY YOU HAVE BEEN PRAYING
IS JUST FINE

Sʜɪᴠᴄʜᴇɪ HᴀBᴇsʜᴛ and translated in Iɴ Pʀᴀɪsᴇ ᴏғ ᴛʜᴇ Bᴀᴀʟ Sʜᴇᴍ Tᴏᴠ by Mintz and Ben Amos.

Chapter Four

Disbelief

SHMUOS VESIPURIM as translated in STORIES OF THE BAAL SHEM TOV by Rabbi Y.Y.Klapholtz.

Chapter Five

PERFECT FAITH AND IMPERFECT TRUTH

A TREASURY OF CHASSIDIC TALES by Rabbi Shlomo Yosef Zevin.

SEEKERS OF SLUMBERING SOULS by Rabbi Moshe Rabin.

HATOMIM as translated in STORIES OF THE BAAL SHEM TOV by Rabbi Y.Y.Klapholtz.

Chapter Six

THE HOLY SHABBOS

STORIES OF THE BAAL SHEM TOV by Rabbi Y.Y.Klapholtz.

Chapter Seven

THE WEDDING BLESSINGS

EXTRAORDINARY CHASSIDIC TALES by Rabbi R.N.Kahn.

Chapter Eight

TWO CANDLES ARE ENOUGH

SEEKER OF SLUMBERING SOULS by Rabbi Moshe Rabin.

Chapter Nine

SINCERE PRAYER

DEVORIN ARAIVIM as translated in STORIES OF THE BAAL SHEM TOV by Rabbi Y.Y.Klapholtz.

Chapter Ten

THE BOOK

STORIES OF THE BAAL SHEM TOV by Rabbi Y.Y.Klapholtz.

THE LIGHT AND FIRE OF THE BAAL SHEM TOV by Yitzhak Buxbaum.

SHIVCHEI HABESHT and translated in IN PRAISE OF THE BAAL SHEM TOV by Mintz and Ben Amos.

Chapter Twelve

THE STORY TELLER

THE STORY TELLER by Rabbi N.Mindel.

SEEKERS OF SLUMBERING SOULS by Rabbi Moshe Rabin.

CLASSIC CHASSIDIC TALES by Meyer Levin.

STORIES OF THE BAAL SHEM TOV by Rabbi Y.Y. Klapholtz.

THE EPISTLE

THE BESHT by Professor Emanuel Etkes.

THE RELIGIOUS THOUGHT OF CHASSIDIM

by Rabbi Norman Lamm.

THE PATH OF THE BAAL SHEM TOV by Rabbi David Sears.

DEDICATIONS

WITH GREAT ADMIRATION AND LOVE,
WE REMEMBER OUR BELOVED MOTHER,
GRANDMOTHER AND
GREAT GRANDMOTHER

CHAVA BAS
MENACHEM MENDEL

MENACHEM AND CHAYA FLANK
AND FAMILY

IN HONOR
OF OUR
CHILDREN
JONATHAN AND SHOSHANA KAUFMAN

....

IN
RECOGNITION OF
A SPECIAL MAN
ON A SPECIAL OCCASION
LARRY WAXMAN
HIS LOVING FAMILY
ORLY AND THE CHILDREN

IN LOVING MEMORY OF
ROSE POLLACK
FROM HER HUSBAND MIKE,
AND HER CHILDREN, GRANDCHILDREN
AND GREAT GRANDCHILDREN

....

DEDICATED IN HONOR OF
OUR
CHILDREN
MAY THE LIGHT OF TORAH SHINE
BRIGHTLY IN THEM
SARAH AND STEVEN ROSEN

TO
BASHA AND TZVI
NACHUS FROM YOUR CHILDREN
THEY SHOULD MERIT TO SEE THE
MOSHIACH
STERNA AND JOSEPH DEITSCH

....

TO MY AMAZING WIFE
ELINOR
AND OUR CHILDREN
RAINA ESTER, TANYA RUTH,
MOSHE ZION AND AARON JOSEF
WITH SO MUCH LOVE AND APPRECIATION
AITAN LEVY

DEAR TZVI AND BASHA
IT IS WITH GREAT PRIDE AND ADMIRATION
THAT WE WISH YOU YASHER KOACH FOR THIS
COMPILATION
OF THE BAAL SHEM TOV STORIES
YOUR FRIENDS THE GREENBERGS
STEVE, EDITH, JULIANA, DAVID,
ALAN & ELISA

....

TO MY WONDERFUL WIFE CYNDI,
WE SHOULD CONTINUE
TO LEARN TORAH TOGETHER
KEN ROLLER

....

WITH DEEP RESPECT WE ACKNOWLEDGE OUR
PARENTS
BENYAMIN BEN SHMUEL OBM
LEYKE BAS YOSEF
ELIYAHU BEN BORIS
LIBE BAS MEIR LOVE,
DAVID BEN BENYAMIN AND MALKA SIMCHA BAS
ELIYAHU
KOTTLER

....

WITH LOVE WE HONOR OUR CHILDREN AND
GRANDCHILDREN
IRENE AND TIBOR ROSENBERG

TO RABBI ZALMAN KAZEN AND REBBETZYN
SHULAMITH KAZEN OF CONGREGATION
ZEMACH ZEDEK:
YOUR TIRELESS DEVOTION TO *YIDDISHKEIT*
AND LOVE FOR ALL JEWS INSPIRE US AND HAS
SET A SHINING EXAMPLE FOR OTHERS TO
EMULATE.YOUR LIVES ARE TRULY A *KIDDUSH
HASHEM.*
WITH MUCH AFFECTION AND RESPECT,
HARVEY AND KAREN KUGELMAN AND FAMILY

....

IN HONOR OF MY WIFE MALKA AND CHILDREN
RIVKA AND PINCHAS
MOSHE ROSENBERG

....

TO OUR WONDERFUL, BELOVED CHILDREN ELAD
ITIEL He shall live, NAAMAH DINAH She shall live,
CHENYA LEAH She shall live, YESHAYAHU DAVID He shall live
MAY YOU ALWAYS KNOW FAITH, LOVE, JOY WITH
LOVE FROM YOUR PARENTS
YOSEF AND SARAH ISRAELI They shall live

WWW.MEZUZAH.NET

Home of the World Wide Mezuzah Campaign

The fundamental goal of The World Wide Mezuzah Campaign is to unify the Jewish people. By fulfilling the mitzvah of Mezuzah, this unity can be accomplished by each Jewish person: man, woman or child. The mitzvah can be easily fulfilled by affixing a Mezuzah on the "Doorpost of Your House or upon Your Gates," as required by Jewish law.

Purchase Mezuzahs written in Israel by a Certified Scribe, then checked by a computer for accuracy and finally checked by a second Certified Scribe before we send it to you. Our Mezuzahs are of a very high quality, and they are beautifully written. They are shipped to you in a Mezuzah case ready to mount on your door.

www.mezuzah.net

The World Wide Mezuzah Campaign.
A project of the Baal Shem Tov Foundation
a 501(c)(3), non-profit organization
www.baalshemtov.com

Baal Shem Tov Times

Spreading the light of the legendary
Kabbalah Master and Mystic
Rabbi Yisrael Baal Shem Tov

-A weekly email publication-

Features:
Baal Shem Tov Story
Torah Baal Shem Tov
Heart of Prayer
Divine Light
Kesser Shem Tov

Subscribe to receive your FREE weekly
e-mail edition at
www.baalshemtov.com

ABOUT THE AUTHOR

TZVI MEIR (Howard M.) Cohn is a Patent and Trademark Attorney (www.CohnPatents.com). He attended Yeshiva Hadar Hatorah in Crown Heights, Brooklyn after completing his university studies in Engineering and Law. While studying at the Yeshiva, he discovered a deep connection to the stories and teachings of the Baal Shem Tov. More recently, he founded the Baal Shem Tov Foundation which is dedicated to spreading the teachings of the Baal Shem Tov throughout the world in order to hasten the coming of the Moshiach. To spread the teachings of the Baal Shem Tov, Tzvi Meir created a website, BaalShemTov.com and publishes a weekly newsletter, The Baal Shem Tov Times. Also, Tzvi Meir initiated the World Wide Mezuzah Campaign (www.Mezuzah.net) as a project of the Baal Shem Tov Foundation. Tzvi Meir gives live presentations of his original music and Baal Shem Tov stories to welcoming audiences.

Made in United States
Troutdale, OR
12/10/2024

26245164R00089